CHRISTOPHER LOWELL,
THE
hassle-free host

CHRISTOPHER LOWELL,
THE
hassle-free host

SUPER-SIMPLE TABLESCAPES AND RECIPES FOR STUNNING PARTIES

CHRISTOPHER LOWELL

with Frances Schultz

clarkson potter/publishers
new york

Published by Clarkson Potter/Publishers, New York, New York.
Member of the Crown Publishing Group, a division of Random House, Inc.
www.crownpublishing.com

CLARKSON N. POTTER is a trademark and POTTER and colophon are registered trademarks of Random House, Inc.

For more information on Christopher Lowell, please visit: ChristopherLowell.com
Christopher Lowell is a registered trademark. Any use of this mark without the written permission of Christopher Lowell
Enterprises, LLC is strictly prohibited.
Christopher Lowell is represented by Daniel J. Levin, Associated Talent Management.

Printed in Japan

Design by Maggie Hinders

Library of Congress Cataloging-in-Publication Data
Lowell, Christopher.
    Christopher Lowell, the hassle-free host : super-simple tablescapes and recipes for stunning parties.
        p. cm.
1. Entertaining. 2. Cookery. 3. Menus. I. Title: Hassle-free host. II. Title.
TX731.L63   2004
642'.4—dc22   2003023300

ISBN 1-4000-4726-9

10 9 8 7 6 5 4 3 2 1

First Edition

THIS BOOK IS DEDICATED to my Nana Belengeri. She came over from Sicily barely able to read or write and poor as a church mouse. She woke every morning at 4:30 to begin the food preparation for the day, before she went off to make brooms for the Fuller Brush Company—back-breaking work. She taught my mother, Josephine, how to cook, preserving classic peasant Italian recipes that I, two generations later, still serve. "Waste not, want not" could have been coined by her. Even eggshells were not discarded but used as soil mulch for my Pop Belengeri's amazing tomato and basil plants. Food was the center of her life. No sooner was the table cleared than the next was being set. By the time she died, she'd owned two houses outright and left her daughter an inheritance. Not bad for a woman who started out with little more than a dream to live in America, the land of opportunity and good produce.

contents

Ridiculously Easy Recipes: 12 GREAT MENUS   89

preface

MY MOTHER, JOSEPHINE, LIKE HER MOTHER, was a self-taught, classic Italian cook who made her kitchen the center of my family's universe. As first-generation Americans, we grew up proud to be offspring of poor Sicilian immigrants. But Jo, may she rest in peace, also used food as a way to communicate. She was a working mom, and time was precious. When she was at home, she was often in the kitchen, so if I wanted to be with her—guess what—that's where I was, too. I can remember sitting up on the counter for our nightly conversations. While she cooked dinner we solved all the world's problems. I know this cemented the life-long bond between us, but it wasn't until many years later that I realized just how much I'd actually learned about preparing great, inexpensive, and memorable meals. Through my time spent watching her, I had not only inadvertently learned the basics but also discovered a love of food in me that burns bright even today. In fact, if I hadn't gone into decorating, I might have actually become a chef. Then I read somewhere that restaurant owners boasted the highest rate of alcoholism of any profession, so I decided to keep that hobby at home (the chef hobby, I mean!).

What I loved about my mom's attitude was that she wasn't pretentious when it came to entertaining. No one cared about her china and stemware. One bite of her veal Parmesan and you were hooked. The laughter and camaraderie came from the shared experience of enjoying her great food. Like her mother's, her food was her gift, which she gave in abundance—and which was consumed with abandon, until we were so full we ached. Belt buckles loosened and shirt fronts splashed with tomato spots were simply evidence of a happily lost battle of the bulge. God bless her. Although there isn't a day I don't miss her, I will always feel connected to her spirit through her recipes. I still have many of her handwritten menus, which are among my prized possessions.

My father, Henry, was a different story. His Bostonian blue-blooded family could not have been further at the other end of the social spectrum. Virginia, his mother and my grandmother (or my Auntie Mame, I should say) lived in an extraordinary eighteenth-century restored mansion. Touted as one of New England's great antiques authorities, she presided over important and valuable collections of tableware she had inherited and accumulated over the years. The bazillion place settings of sterling silver, lined up like soldiers on either side of her gold-trimmed chargers, bore hallmarks of the likes of Paul Revere. Her dinner parties were rather formal affairs, to say the least. A wrongly used utensil or ill-placed elbow was met with a withering eye.

I had to live with my grandmother on the other side of the Piscataqua River, in Portsmouth, New Hampshire, in order to go to the nearby public school of choice. She and my step-grandfather, Professor William G. Hennesy, were quite the duo. I learned endlessly from the two of them. He, a doctor of letters, with friends including Winston Churchill, and she, a legendary arbiter of good taste whose ancestors' portraits hang in the White House, kept me on my toes. On rainy days, Virginia would teach me how to set a table piece by piece. It was an all-day affair. Like Emily Post, I was educated in the proper school of etiquette. Years later, as I entered "society" (or was thrown into it), this training proved invaluable.

Over the years I've really come to appreciate the contrast between both families' approaches to food and entertaining and how it has given me a fabulous range of experiences from which to draw. I'll bet your family background and traditions have too. Think about it, and about how you might carry on that legacy.

introduction

why bother to entertain?

UNLESS YOU GREW UP ON THE MOON, chances are there was a kitchen in the place you grew up, and chances are there was someone in it doing something most of the time. It may even be that some of your earliest impressions of family are of people or things that happened in the kitchen or around the dinner table—back when families actually used to have meals together around the dinner table. Anybody out there remember that? I sure do. And I think something in all of us wants to have that again. Oh, I know it's not practical in this day and age to have a formal sit-down dinner every night, but don't you think there is still something appealing and deeply satisfying about gathering friends and family and sharing a meal? It's a way to connect to those we love, a way to reach out, to learn from each other, to grow, to make new friends and keep the old, as the song goes. And in this crazy world we live in, I think we need all of that we can get, don't you? The reason I'm saying all this is that as I think back about my family and what I guess I would call my "history of entertaining," I realize it had a lot to do with how I interacted with my family and friends growing up and how I formed relationships. And when I think about how important these interactions are, I realize how important it is to continue to entertain—and to eat with—my family and friends today.

HOW THIS BOOK HAPPENED

IN 1999 I DECIDED to broaden the scope of my television show to include in-home entertaining. As entertaining is a favorite pastime of mine, I naturally thought it would be met with great enthusiasm by our viewers. Well, I was partly right. Being the very first to use the word *tablescape,* a decade earlier (yep, that was me), I had been known for my imaginative table settings. This skill made for great TV. The cooking, however, did not. After a season of having some of the world's foremost chefs and celebrity restaurateurs grace my chopping block, the viewers rioted. "If we wanted to cook, we'd watch the Food Network," they hollered. And that seemed to be the general consensus. So we kept the party-planning and 86'd the recipes. Then—go figure—as the shows continued in reruns, we received thousands of requests for my recipes. The other sought-after entertaining tips were from author, host, editor, and all-around fabulous gal Frances Schultz. Her chic good looks and easy Southern charm captured my viewers' hearts. Her approach to entertaining was confident, approachable, and elegantly casual. Later, in the comfort of her stylish Manhattan pied-à-terre, I witnessed her ability to pull a dinner party together literally in minutes. People dropped by unannounced and were welcomed with a great big "Hey y'all!" From what seemed a bottomless pantry, great food appeared from nowhere. When we all left, the apartment was spotless. In jammies and bathrobes later at my home in Los Angeles, we started dreaming up the idea for what we hoped would be a terrific (if we do say so ourselves) YOU-CAN-DO-IT entertaining book! And unlike any other. . . .

WHAT MAKES A GOOD PARTY (AHEM, AND WHAT DOESN'T . . .)

BETWEEN GIVING AND ATTENDING, Frances and I figured that between us we'd done the party thing thousands of times. But why do some people's parties work while others fail? We've seen guests who just sit there like lumps, and we've seen the other extreme. You know, where Mr. Livewire tells the one about the traveling salesman and your poor mother-in-law nearly chokes? Or when your old college roommate's new boyfriend does his take on a dance number from *La Cage aux Folles*? Um-hmm, you know what I mean. And then there was the time when we walked into the kitchen—it was getting *awfully* late—and wanted to see if we could help, only to find the hostess dissolved in tears because the soufflé had collapsed, and so had she.

Are you with me? Some parties are beautifully orchestrated, while others leave the guests thinking, "What *were* they thinking?"

We giggled and compared notes and agreed that there was nothing more embarrassing than putting your guests (a future in-law, business associate, or potential friend) through a dull or out-of-control evening. Geez, no wonder you don't entertain. But start getting that notion out of your head right now, sister.

WHAT HOLDS YOU BACK? (AND WHAT WE'RE GOING TO DO ABOUT IT!)

WE REALIZED THAT BECAUSE of this pressure, many people don't even attempt to entertain. In fact, for lots of folks, the actual word *entertaining* is terrifying. It conjures up a mental image of the host on stage, drenched with sweat, sautéing as fast as he can. We wanted to change that. If we could get folks to think of a party as entertain*ment* rather than entertain-*ing,* understanding that the host is supposed to be entertained too, then we knew we'd have something—and hey, so would you.

We then realized that we were perceived as proficient hosts and shared secrets between us, which, if exposed (gasp), might tarnish our reputations. Yep, we cheat. That's right. Big fat cheaters, both of us. So sue us. We're proud because we learned early on that it's not about gourmet but rather good times. Entertaining was our way of making friends, not impressing them—and yet we did. As we began to confess, looking over our shoulders for enemy spies, we started this book.

Would we dare to tell America that a box of Stouffer's mac and cheese, when layered with canned peppers and Stilton cheese scooped into individual ramekins, could be, and was, passed off as *Pâtes et Fromage aux Poivrons*? You bet your French accent it could. (Not that we'd really call it that, by the way, but you see our point?) Would we dare to divulge a gourmet salad made by opening three cans? Oh dear. Could we, if word got out, hold our heads up ever again? The answer was YES. Because we'd been there, done that.

We'd watched very rich people entertain very poorly. We'd seen those of meager resources give the best parties ever. It wasn't about the money, social status, or culinary skill; it was about the confidence, spirit, and graciousness that made for a good time. And time is a more precious commodity than ever.

DOES THIS SOUND LIKE YOU?

WE'VE HEARD IT A MILLION TIMES. It goes something like this: So, you finally decide on a Monday that it's time you had a payback party—that is, if you ever want to be invited anywhere again. You start to plan; it gets too big, too ambitious, and too expensive. By Tuesday, you scale back on everything while your list on the legal pad grows and you fill with anxiety. By Wednesday, it's a joyless chore and your self-esteem plummets. By Thursday, you're chickening out; and by Friday, out of sheer terror, you've talked yourself into the only solution—cancel the damn thing! You'll go get a root canal instead! Who needs that kind of pressure?

It's frustration at its worst—especially since your next-door neighbor has these really cool impromptu parties that seem to erupt out of nowhere, and she has as much fun as her guests.

If this sounds familiar, this book's for you. It's a step-by-step guide to having fun at your own party while still being able to pay your mortgage and not your shrink.

HERE WE GO!

AND WE GO BEYOND THE CLICHÉS . . . you know . . . stay organized. Don't be overly ambitious. If you're having fun, so will they. Blah, blah, blah. This books gets down and dirty.

Our humorous but practical "cheat where you can" and "let's not and say we did" attitude makes this book not only a great resource but also a great read, even if you've never turned on the oven.

But don't be fooled, this is not just a cookbook—not totally, anyway. That would assume you actually liked to cook and fancied yourself a budding gourmet. It's not an etiquette guide. That would assume you're dying to eat "pinky up." And best of all, it's not a "look at the pretty pictures of a soirée on the porch of a multimillion-dollar estate in East Hampton" kind of book, either.

Christopher Lowell, the Hassle-Free Host is a practical "don't sweat it, you'll be fine" road map to hosting a winning event, planned or spontaneous. From classic buffet to casual potluck to intimate sit-down to feeding the masses, this book will help you set the stage so when your audience stands, it's an ovation and not an escape.

GUERRILLA GOURMET: THE ART AND WARFARE OF IMPROMPTU ENTERTAINING

ARE YOU READY to receive your mantra? Listen carefully: Shake, open, and pour—and God bless ready-made! Now repeat after me. . . .

It used to be that in order to make a decent meal, everything had to be made from scratch. That fact alone made in-home entertaining a daunting task. Today, with technology and the food industry's finally catching on to the fact that June Cleaver left a long time ago, you'd be surprised at what's available ready-made or ready to assemble at most supermarkets. It used to be you paid through the nose for "cheating" by way of specially ordered foods at pricey boutiques where potatoes were individually wrapped like Christmas presents and the cooks signed affidavits swearing them to secrecy.

Now even the corner Piggly-Wiggly in Podunk carries ready-made and packaged foods that require little or no preparation. I mean, when was the last time you made a cake from scratch? Why bother when the holy trinity of Duncan (Hines), Sara (Lee), and Betty (Crocker) has it down to a science? And let's not forget about T.P.D. (the Pillsbury Doughboy) or my favorite weekend retreat, Pepperidge Farm. Together these gourmet technowizards have given us their blessing simply to shake, open, and pour. Love it. It's also the approach to this book. Now we can not do it and say we did in half the time. How cool is that?

The trick is knowing the shortcuts so your guests at least feel like you slaved away just for them, because they are sooo special. But listen, as Frances always says, "Who gives a . . . ?" (Oops, I better not say *exactly* what Frances says.) "Look," she says, "people are just happy to be invited and even happier not to be doing the work themselves. Put yourself in your guest's place. Would you really go home grumbling if there weren't rose petals frozen into each and every ice cube? If the desserts weren't topped with miniature spun-sugar butterflies with wings that really worked? Right, I thought so. So get on with it, honey."

Now I know there are genuine foodies out there who are cringing as they read this. Even *I* love tackling complicated gourmet dishes on the weekends WHEN I HAVE TIME! But time is as much the point as the expertise. So for you persnickety purists with time to burn, all I can say is put this book back on the shelf and step away from the counter.

ENTERTAINING IS TO *MAKE* FRIENDS, NOT IMPRESS THEM!

YOU'VE HEARD ME SAY to decorate with your heart and not your ego? Well, the same applies to entertaining. What we've learned over the years is that flavor should never be compromised for presentation, and guests should never be victims of their host's ego. Sometimes we feel we can't live up to others' expectations or that we couldn't top a party we just attended. All this is that ol' bugaboo called *ego,* and all it does is amplify your fear. And where there's fear there's no creativity. Gee, where have I heard that before?

Being a good cook and being a clever cook are two different things. Your goal is not to convince your guests of your culinary skills but to host a gathering where you can facilitate goodwill, friendship, generosity, and love—all the things you can do better at home than at Sushi-Rama-A-Go-Go or wherever, because otherwise you'd just dine out. Entertaining in your home allows those whom you think need to know you better a place, and just as importantly a context, in which to do it.

Great parties are not conspicuously planned but instead seem just to happen, as though there were no set agenda. And that's exactly the point. When you've invited friends for drinks and nobody wants to go home, it's spontaneous and genuine to say, "Hey, stay and let's have dinner!" It really is great to be able to do that, and it's a far cry better than a calculated evening contrived to curry favor from your unsuspecting guests.

People are smart. They know when they're being manipulated, and that sense can weigh down a party before it ever gets off the ground, not to mention derail a potentially wonderful relationship or bonding experience. So lighten up and put your ego in your pocket. Okay?

If we are how we live, then our homes should be a reflection of who we are. Our ability to make others comfortable should pay homage to how we live in this space we call home.

There's no question that when we open our doors to the world outside we can feel vulnerable and suddenly open to criticism. This might be because we're inviting the wrong people in. Uh-huh. Sorry to be so blunt, but there are folks I'd meet for a meal in a restaurant whom I wouldn't invite home to an intimate dinner. A raucous "crammed to the rafters" event, maybe, but not to an evening where we could all let our hair down (or in my case what there is left of it). And that's okay. I've got plenty of acquaintances I feel comfortable with on a superficial basis. They're fun but would never become part of my adopted family.

For that matter, some of my own real family I'd rather meet in a public place than host at home. That's okay too. A dinner party is no place to throw potentially good friends in with the goofballs you might have inherited. It's a recipe for disaster. Now certainly weddings and anniversaries can't be helped, but even then, if there's a lot of baggage, those events should be held on neutral ground.

The kind of entertaining we're giving you the courage to do is for people you believe could enhance and bring joy to your life, and you theirs. Get it? All righty then. Here are a few more things you might want to address:

DIET, SCHMIET!

YOUR DINNER PARTY is no place to establish a federal nutrition clinic. People don't come to your home to maintain their diet; they come as an excuse to *break* it! Certainly you should be health-aware, but a little indulgence will make your party memorable. More people remember a great and decadent dessert than they do the actual entrée. Besides, now you have an excuse to break your diet too. Who knew? This is a time to celebrate! Cut loose with both your appetite and your belt buckle. If you want someone's kid to like you, you bribe him with candy, right? Well, who's to say your guests won't be a little more forthcoming with their good wishes over a piece of chocolate mud pie? That kind of agenda I don't mind. 'Nuf said.

MATCHMAKER

KNOW THE ATTITUDE OF YOUR PARTY before you throw money at it. Here's what I mean:
ASK YOURSELF, "What would the kind of people I'm inviting feel most comfortable with?"
- A quiet sit-down dinner, with two or three other couples?
- A larger roaming buffet, where people wander and mingle as they please?
- A combination of buffet and seated dinner, where guests
  serve themselves and sit where they like?
- A combination buffet and seated dinner, where I plan the seating?

AND THEN DECIDE who's coming:
- Couples only?
- A mix of single and married?
- Adults but no children?
- Adults with children?

THE QUIET SIT-DOWN

The quiet sit-down, with four to eight people, seems to be appropriate for people who are good conversationalists. Meaning, no one would be put on the spot or have to endure awkward gaps of silence. This is the ideal setting in which to offer and exchange ideas. People who are naturally poised and comfortable in their own skins fare well here.

THE ROAMING BUFFET

The roaming buffet is appropriate for a larger and more mixed group. You may have people you know well and others you might want to observe to find out if you *want* to get to know them. A roaming buffet allows you to cater to a variety of tastes and allows guests to graze as they like. Because it's sort of a potluck atmosphere and people are standing and moving around, this kind of party can be a good icebreaker. It's nonthreatening, and guests who are self-conscious may come and go as they please. Rather than one big Rose Bowl–sized food table, I suggest strategically placing grazing stations around the house. Made up of small, separate tables, these stations allow for pairing foods with themes—a salsa table, a fruit and cheese table, a dessert table, to name a few—and become destination points during the party. This encourages traffic flow and is a great way to show off different parts of your house.

BUFFET WITH RANDOM SEATING

The buffet with random table seating is really a mix of roaming and seated. The breaking-bread-together aspect is still there, and you can still cater to a variety of tastes in an informal way. It's a self-serve and sit-next-to-whom-you'd-like kind of deal. This works best when everyone at the table has enough in common that no matter whom they sit next to, the conversation will flow.

SEATED BUFFET

The buffet where you assign the seating—the *placement,* as the French call it —is an ideal way for you to put people together who might not know each other but who you think might enjoy each other. This also gives you a chance to separate couples and cronies and keep inside conversation to a minimum. You don't want anyone to feel left out.

The buffet style in general is less stressful to all concerned, especially the host. Room-temperature foods can be put out in advance, and your job is simply to replenish. The table can be set in advance, and the pressure to serve your guests individually and keep things hot and the kitchen clean and the plates garnished—WHEW—is eliminated. Love that!

P.S. I know I said this isn't an etiquette book, and it isn't, but since most of etiquette is just common sense, I thought this worth mentioning here. A lot of people, and I mean people who ought to know better, get this wrong, and it drives Frances crazy. All right, Miss Fancy Pants, here it is: If you are serving individually, or you have hired someone else to serve, the form is to serve from the left and take away from the right. That's because most people are right-handed and less likely to fling the plate out of the server's hands when it's presented from the left.

BUTT WHAT ABOUT SEATING?

If you are doing the roaming buffet thing, or a larger cocktail party, chances are you have more people than you have places to seat them. Or you've invited twelve and your living room seats only eight. All the better, I say. I don't like the idea of cluttering a room with folding chairs. It's a party, not a town meeting. Besides, guests all lined up staring at each other does not encourage mingling. If the room seems just a tiny bit crowded, that's good. It says, "Oooh, something's *happening* here," you know? People can sit on arms of sofas, or simply stand, bar-fashion. This makes for a more integrated group by the time dinner is served. That said, do make an exception for older guests or those with special needs who may not be prepared or able to perch on the arms of sofas or to stand. In these cases, a straight-back dining chair—which is easy to get in and out of—is just what you (and they) need.

INVITATIONS?

There are two thoughts here. On the one hand, a formal invitation denotes a formal affair. It builds expectations in the minds of the guests and so naturally creates certain expectations of your party skills. I think they work for formal occasions where it is vital that special people are available. Weddings, birthdays, bar mitzvahs, and other special events warrant an invitation. For a party of four to eight, however, I think invitations are a little pretentious and take the spontaneity and casualness out of the event. For more than eight, you could go either way. Frances says she likes the idea of sending invitations, but getting around to it is usually another matter. We know all about that, don't we? When she does send them, they are usually slightly wacky and not at all serious, just to set the mood or establish a theme for the evening.

An e-mail or a phone call works well, too, I think. It allows you then and there to know who can and cannot come, to ask your guests what they like, and to establish dress, booze, and food issues. "Lula May, by all means wear your tiara. And are you still drinking honeysuckle wine? Because I'll be sure to have some if you are. And now tell me, Lula May, does Lawrence's head still swell up like a watermelon if he eats crabmeat?" you may ask. Nothing is worse than serving stuffed pork to a vegetarian couple, or fish to someone who breaks out in hives at the sight of it. Who knows? Someone might even volunteer to bring a dish. But if you allow one guest to bring a covered dish, then it is best to let the other guests know so they don't feel bad coming empty-handed. A nice bottle of wine or a bag of ice can be just as helpful as an entrée.

WHAT ABOUT KIDS?

If you decide to do a no-children event, then let everyone know in advance so that little Bobby doesn't end up monopolizing what was supposed to be an adult evening. Or an awkward teenager doesn't sulk herself into oblivion and put a major drag on your shindig. Or one of your racier friends doesn't say something not quite ready for prime time and someone's mother never speaks to you again. Are you with me?

With children, confine the occasion to morning, afternoon, or early evening, but give your nonparenting friends the heads-up. Don't assume everyone adores your little Gertrude, and more importantly, don't assume they want to spend that particular day or evening with her. Rule of thumb, if your child is too young to behave well in a restaurant, then a home party setting will be a mistake, and that could be an understatement.

Here again, the more you know how you'd like the event to go, the better you'll be able to plan it.

TABLE SHAPE

My favorite shape of dinner table is round. This assures that there is really no head of the table, and everyone can see everyone else. I used to keep a large plywood round in my basement to convert my rectangle harvest table into a round one at a moment's notice. Who cares what's under the tablecloth?

Having said that, Frances offers another opinion. While she loves round dinner tables and has one herself, she thinks a rectangle is more conducive to conversation. "With a round table, you are pretty much limited to talking to the person on either side of you, or you're shouting across the roast beef. With a rectangle, you have the people on either side as well as the ones across, who are a little closer than shouting distance."

She has a point. If you have an option, experiment with both. If you don't, it's no big deal. Frances doesn't even *own* a rectangular table, for heaven's sake.

I'LL HAVE TEE MARTUNIES: THE ART OF THE BAR

Speaking of the bar, you need to keep a few things in mind. There should always be options for both those who partake and those who don't. Those who are offended by those who do should be warned in advance. If you know for sure it's going to be an issue, just don't invite them, or invite them another time, like breakfast. (Like never, says Frances.)

My typical bar setup looks like this, for a group of six to twelve:

WINE AND SPIRITS
- 3 to 4 bottles white wine
- 3 to 4 bottles red wine

- 1 gallon vodka
- 1 liter or fifth scotch
- 1 liter or fifth rum
- 1 liter or fifth gin
- 1 liter or fifth bourbon

MIXERS

- Three 32-ounce bottles tonic
- Three 32-ounce bottles soda or sparkling water
- Three 32-ounce bottles cola
- Three 32-ounce bottles ginger ale
- Three 32-ounce bottles diet soda
- $\frac{1}{2}$ gallon orange juice
- $\frac{1}{2}$ gallon cranberry juice
- Olives, lemons, and limes

For afternoon events, add:
- Beer or ale
- Bloody Mary mix
- Celery, Tabasco sauce, salt, and pepper

We've found that most prudent people have two drinks during the cocktail hour with hors d'oeuvre. Some will switch to wine with the meal and champagne with dessert. But many will not. So don't be offended if guests who don't or can't mix beg off.

Obviously, you tailor this inventory to your own and your guests' preferences. These days we find fewer people drinking mixed drinks and more people drinking wine. To be safe, have more than you need. It doesn't go bad, you know, and it's such a drag to run out of something.

Locate your bar away from high-traffic areas like hallways, kitchens, or dining areas. A draped card table is fine, by the way. And on a nice evening, a setup out on a deck is even better. Beware the bottleneck! People always, and we mean *always,* congregate around the bar—there and the kitchen—so you'd better put the bar where you want them to go. (And organize your kitchen so they'll at least stay out of your way!)

There are differing opinions on this, but Frances is fanatical about it: If you have more than twenty-five people, you might need to have more than one bar. You could have one full-service bar, with a bartender, and have another self-serve, maybe with wine and beer only. "Nothing's worse than having to fight for a drink," she says, "or to wait forever for one."

She'll often have a tray of white wine and sparkling water right at the door for her guests to pick up as they come in. That eases the initial strain on the bar, and as the rush subsides, visits to the bar are staggered and it's not a problem—as long as it's the visits staggering and not the guests!

If you don't have a bartender, solicit a friend to help you serve small numbers of guests. For bigger affairs, lead your guests to a well-laid-out self-serve bar and let them know where everything is, including the predinner snacks.

YOU RANG, MADAME?

To have or not to have help—that may be a question. Yes, it's an extra expense, but it's worth it if there's any way your budget can handle it. Just getting the plates and glasses picked up and the dishwasher loaded is a tremendous bonus. You don't have to hire Jeeves. Maybe you have a babysitter who wouldn't mind helping out in the kitchen for a few hours. Or maybe a friend's son is home from college and might like to make a few extra bucks tending bar (but ask him to lose the Smashing Pumpkins T-shirt). Or do you know a part-time housekeeper, or a friend's housekeeper? Ask around. My point is that your help doesn't have to be a high-priced waiter from a catering company. Improvise! That's what we're all about here.

CHECK, PLEASE

How much should you spend per person? First off, if you're on a serious budget, steer toward events like pasta parties, potluck parties, and soup parties, with little to no bar. Wine and liquor expenses add up quickly, and keeping them to a minimum will really help keep costs down.

For a formal, well-produced evening with all the trimmings, caterers tell us to be prepared to spend, per head, as much as you would in a medium-priced restaurant. That's about $25 to $30 a head. That's not to say you have to, but by the time you add the extras, don't be surprised if it comes out to $30 a pop or more. That said, this per-head price should provide for a high-end, five-star evening. Meaning you'll get the medium price tag for what would have been prohibitive in a five-star eating establishment. So that ain't all bad.

AMBIANCE AND ENCHANTÉ

I SPY

Streamline your surfaces of clutter for the evening. Room dandruff can get in the way and rob you, your guests, and your rooms of their function. Walk through your house as your guests would to be sure that what they see is okay with you. If there are photos, books, bills, etc., that could be misconstrued, then they should be stored where prying eyes won't find them.

And I hate to say it, but the same goes for the medicine cabinet. Shocking but true. Curiosity may kill the cat, but that is no reason to announce, however inadvertently, that the Visa bill is overdue, little Johnny is not doing well in math, and you take a sleeping pill every now and then. Also remove anything that is easily knocked over or irreplaceable. One way to ruin a party is to make a guest feel bad because you didn't take the necessary precautions. No one is accident-proof. Chances are something will eventually break or spill, so have cleaning products handy (and that means the kind of club soda *with* sodium), and don't make a big deal over it.

MUSIC

Music should be upbeat as guests arrive and transition to dinner music that is more instrumental and background. Then reflective classics after dinner will help the party wind down to a tranquil conclusion. Keep the volume low enough so people can hear each other without raising their voices. They came to visit, not flex their vocal cords. Now, if your idea of reflective classics is "Disco Inferno"—sometimes these things happen—that's the time to turn the music up. Just try not to disturb the neighbors.

The trick to music is to keep it going. Selecting your playlist in advance will assure your party doesn't come to a screeching halt when the music stops, unless you're playing musical chairs. (Hmm, that could be fun, too. . . .)

The idea is to create three different moods to underscore the evening for heightened emotional effect, like a movie score enhances the plot.

TV?

No.

Unless your do is structured around a scheduled event, like election night or the Super Bowl, keep the television off. It offends people who came to get to know you better. It's the ultimate distraction and robs the event of that special intimacy you're trying to create.

LIGHTING

Lighting should be romantic—dimmed and cozy. Who can create a mood in a cafeteria? Unless they are on dimmers, overhead lights should be turned off. Task lights and lamps should be on low. If there is only one setting for a lamp, replace a high-wattage bulb with a low-wattage one, say 25 watts. Remember that when all lamps are on, even at low wattage, all that light adds up.

Get those uplights on. Nothing creates mood and intimacy like shadow. I recommend candles dispersed evenly around the room. The flicker of candlelight is flattering and atmospheric. When in doubt, use more rather than less. In fact, I think you simply cannot overdo it here.

CHEERS!

When everyone's arrived and has a beverage in hand, you as the host may want to offer a welcoming toast and let your guests know what to expect as the evening progresses. It should go something like this: "Welcome to our home. Having you all here in one place reminds us of how great life can be. Cocktails in the garden will be one hour followed by dinner on the terrace. Later we will be serving dessert and after-dinner drinks inside in the living room. So enjoy."

If you feel a toast will slow the party, then as you greet your guests and show them to the bar, you can simply let them know the drill individually. This clues the guests that they're in competent hands and that the event has been well thought out. They are then free to relax knowing they'll be well taken care of.

ARE YOU READY?

I KNOW MUCH OF WHAT I've said is common sense, but without a checklist to remind you, flubbing these details can kill a great time. The more planning in advance, the more fun in the present. Sometimes we get so hung up on the food that we forget the rest of the evening. Helloooo.

LET'S PARTY! HOW THIS BOOK WORKS

TOTALLY DOABLE TABLESCAPES

This section shows you quick and easy ways to tablescape everything from buffets to formal sit-downs to grazing stations. We've tried to keep these visuals non-room-specific and more conceptual to make adaptation to your own house a breeze. The devices we use to create table drama are inexpensive but rich in creating a wonderful memory for your guests. We've kept it simple and versatile so you can customize each setting to your house, your stuff, and your particular needs.

You will also see ideas for invitations and menus. But remember while they may read chi-chi and taste fabulous, they are pure, achievable cheating at its best! Accompanying how-to's will give you versatile tablescaping props to keep on hand as you develop your in-home entertaining arsenal. Follow us step by step, or mix and match as you see fit.

RIDICULOUSLY EASY RECIPES

This part of the book provides super-simple recipes that are foolproof, and this is what separates this book from others. Few steps mean minimal prep time. Durable, do-ahead dishes mean you don't exhaust yourself at the last minute trying to get the food to come out right, all at the right time. Sound like your kind of cooking? Thought so.

Now I use the word *cooking* rather loosely here. Don't tell Emeril, but whenever possible we use or adapt store-bought ingredients, so the emphasis of the recipe is on assembly rather than actual cooking. Again, this will reduce time spent in the kitchen and clue you in to stockable pantry items you can rally at a moment's notice.

So learn from us old party hounds. We've made all the mistakes already—and those we haven't made ourselves, we've observed. We've learned, more than anything, that it is the spirit of celebration that must be preserved. Entertaining is simply a reason to connect, bond, and make lifelong friends. Besides, you gotta eat, right? When you keep an easy smile on your face and a true desire to share in your heart, people will find any visit to your home an event, whether the party is big or small, planned or not.

See? Now you really can do this!

petal pushers

asian zen squared

crystal blue persuasion

bountiful country feast

veggie-table chic

tin-talizing picnic

grass roots

pizza party

bamboozled

fireside chat

a night at the opera

ballroom classics

PLEASE DON'T EAT THE DAISIES • EVERYTHING'S COMING UP ROSES

let's party

Setting a great table should be a labor of love. While at a glance the following tablescapes appear spectacular, look closer. What you'll see are lots of ordinary household items put to *extra*ordinary use. You'll see that the tablescapes in progress may look sketchy at best, but that once the food, flowers, and candles are added, everything looks fantastic. We did this purposely so you wouldn't freak out midway. Each setting has a detailed list of the things I used, but feel free to substitute whatever you have on hand—and I mean it! If you get caught up in exact translations, then you haven't heard a word I've said. Got that? Use our tablescapes as launching points for your own.

Here's how we've tried to make that easy for you: For the most part, we intentionally stayed away from fine silver and pattern-specific dinnerware. Everything was purchased at mass-market national chains—we stayed away from the chi-chi specialty stores. By keeping the focus on texture, solid colors, simple containers, and make-it-yourself lifts and levels, much of what we've used can be reused again and again. Note how we've done a lot of mixing and matching. Don't be afraid! Do it with confidence, but be deliberate and consistent.

A tablescape should be balanced and functional. Remember that height and scale are what create drama, so when in doubt, go higher! And as in interior design, the eye always goes to color. Many of the tables we show you are done on simple plywood, which can be stored when not in use. So you see, it's not about the table, love, it's about what you *do* on it.

Most of these tablescapes can be shopped for and prepped way in advance and assembled in less than an hour tops! So get most of it done while the heat is off. That way you'll have time to play because, hey, that's all this is about—having fun!

At the end of this section, we even show you how to throw your own fancy shindigs for big crowds and multiple tables. If it seems too ambitious at first, let the fact that it can save you thousands be your motivation.

Once you see the delight and sense of wonder on your guests' faces as they come to your table, you'll be hooked on tablescaping!

Oh, and don't forget to check our super-simple menus and recipes, too. Even if you've never stepped foot in a kitchen, you'd be surprised at how easy the food thing can be. Now you really can do it!

WITH A GRAIN OF SALT . . .

. . . IS HOW YOU SHOULD take our lists of what you'll need. Our lists are really suggestions. We know you may not have or want to bother with buying all the stuff we show here. Use what you have! Improvise! Whatever you do will be great just because *you're doing it*— you know? You're making the effort. You're getting people together. And that's what really counts.

petal pushers

This tablescape proves that one simple idea executed with symmetry and in mass can dazzle even the most discriminating guest. The key is to use identical containers and only one or two kinds of flowers, but lots of 'em. We cheated on the tablecloth and just used fabric right off the bolt. Because we needed lots of flower petals here, inexpensive carnations fit the bill—literally.

WHAT YOU CAN DO WITH THIS:
Springtime luncheon or dinner
Wedding or anniversary luncheon
Sunday brunch, just because
Baby shower
Dining al fresco

. . . OR BY THE BOOK:
Brunch for a Bunch, page 92
Lunch on the Sundeck, page 98
Al Fresco Feast, page 112
Fresh Summer Favorites, page 118

HERE'S WHAT YOU'LL NEED:

3 yards fabric

Ten 4-inch-square glass containers

Ten 15-inch white candles

10 small candleholders

3 dozen carnations

1 dozen accent flowers

Florist's clay (a sticky claylike material you buy in rolls at florist shops and hardware stores) or any moldable adhesive material, such as Duco Stik-Tak™

6 votive candles and holders

Six 12- to 14-inch squares (depending on the size of your plates) particleboard or Masonite

Pale pink latex paint

6 white cloth napkins, starched and ironed

Everyday flatware and china

YOU CAN DO IT!

WE CHOSE A COLOR SCHEME of dusty rose and chartreuse. Just drape the table with fabric and create a hedge down the center by lining up ten inexpensive square glass containers (most florist shops sell these for around $8 each).

With a piece of sticky florist's clay, affix the small candleholders to the center of the bottom of each container, then put in the 15-inch tapers. The candleholders don't need to match because they'll be covered with petals later on.

As an alternative to conventional placemats, you can have the hardware store cut six squares of particleboard, as we did. Paint them pale pink and let them dry. These become the base for building the place setting, which might include a charger, which is optional, and whatever you need for the first course, the main course, and your dessert.

Place the chargers (if using) on the square mats and arrange the napkins in the wine or water glasses. If the napkins are crisply starched, they'll add a nice amount of height to the table. If they're not, they'll sort of flop over, but that's okay, too.

Set the rest of the table with stainless flatware, mix-and-match glasses, and everyday china. You can do that, right?

Save this part for last so the flowers will be as fresh as possible: With scissors, cut the petals from each whole flower where the petals meet the stem and fill the containers to about an inch from the top. Now you can stop here if you're looking for a minimal effect, or . . .

. . . add chartreuse bachelor buttons for a little contrast and because they don't need water to last through a dinner party. If you'd like to use a more delicate—as in perishable—flower, place each stem in an individual vial (available from the florist) and bury it in the other petals.

For the votive candles, consider using them in the color of your second flower to carry that color through the tablescape. If not, white is always fine, too. We used one at each place setting.

WHATEVER YOU DO, be deliberate. In this case, it's symmetry and strength in numbers—arranging objects in mass—that do the trick.

COLOR YOUR WORLD (THE BEST WAY)

THE EYE GOES to color, so spread it evenly around the table for visual balance.

DON'T BE AFRAID . . .

. . . TO MIX AND MATCH, as long as each category of item is the same. For example, the style of the wineglasses might be different from the water glasses, but all the wineglasses should be the same and all the water glasses the same. Ditto the plates. You get the idea.

I WILL REMIND YOU ONCE AGAIN THAT CANDLELIGHT ON A TABLE ADDS SPARKLE AND ANIMATION AT ANY TIME OF THE DAY. IN FACT, I OFTEN HAVE LIT CANDLES ON A TABLE FOR A LUNCHEON BECAUSE THE VERY PRESENCE OF THEM HELPS TO SET A SPECIAL MOOD. CANDLES ARE ESPECIALLY GOOD IF YOUR PARTY STARTS AT, SAY, FOUR O'CLOCK IN THE AFTERNOON AND YOU DON'T EXPECT DESSERT TO WRAP UP UNTIL AFTER THE SUN GOES DOWN. JUST KEEP IN MIND, IT CAN BE A TAD AWKWARD TO GET UP IN THE MIDDLE OF A PARTY AND LIGHT THE CANDLES IN FRONT OF THE GUESTS. IN GENERAL, I THINK CANDLES ARE ALWAYS THE FINISHING TOUCH. AND THE MORE, THE BETTER.

asian zen squared

The Asian Zen look is appropriate for just about any kind of sit-down affair, whether you're serving Asian food or not. Here again, a single element used in quantity is a design strategy that is both flexible and dynamic. By using simple square glass containers, you keep your floral bill low even as the visual drama escalates.

So there you have it—simple, easy, sophisticated, versatile, and unisex enough to impress your most discriminating guest. And best of all, the inexpensive props you buy can be used again and again. Love that!

THIS WOULD WORK FOR LOTS OF OCCASIONS:
Romantic dinner
Banquet for the masses
Dinner for the boss
Cocktail party
Instant party with take-out

. . . OR BY THE BOOK:
Bollywood Boulevard, page 160
Fancy-Schmancy, page 166

YOU CAN DO IT!

SPRAY THE INTERIOR of the glass containers with black Krylon spray paint and let dry overnight. Often a few light coats are better then one thick coat, which can drip. Once sprayed, invert the containers on newspaper while still wet, so they'll drain.

Cover the tabletop by stretching vinyl or fabric tightly over the top and securing it underneath for a clean, tailored look. If you are using your existing table, duct tape will do the job and can be removed without damage. (If the tape leaves a bit of sticky residue, you can remove it with Goo-Gone.) If you're using a plywood top, use a staple gun if you've got one.

Place matchstick, bamboo, or grasscloth placemats end to end down the table's center. Placemats are just as good as—if not better than—an actual table runner because you can use them for other purposes. Either way, make sure the fabric is attached snugly to the table.

Arrange your now painted and dried containers down the center of the table atop the placemats. To avoid them looking too lined up like little soldiers, go for a scattered, random effect. You might want to play around with the arrangement until you get one that pleases your eye. But don't sweat! Once you add the candles and flowers, trust me, it will look great. Be sure to leave upright the containers that will hold flowers; invert the others to act as lifts, levels, and candleholders. Just remember to disperse the flowers and candles evenly down the table for visual balance.

Now it's time to place water in the cubes you've designated to hold your flowers. Then place your candles on the cubes you've designated to act as votives.

Arrange your flowers, cutting them short enough so you see very little stem—mostly just the flower blossom. At this point you can simply set the table and stop there for a clean, tailored effect, or . . .

. . . for a little more whimsy, scatter a bag of green glass tumbled pebbles to break up the line between the placemats and the black tablecloth. Your centerpiece is now complete.

HERE'S WHAT YOU'LL NEED:

Fifteen to twenty 2-, 3-, and 4-inch-square glass containers

Black Krylon spray paint

3–4 yards black plastic vinyl or black poly-silk, or simply a black tablecloth

Duct tape or staple gun

5–6 rattan or grasscloth placemats from an Asian import store (like Pier 1)

18 "architectural" flowers, such as protea (shown) or bromeliads

A few handfuls of polished pebbles, green glass or black (available in craft stores)

Twelve 2-inch chartreuse votive candles and small votive holders

Everyday flatware

Napkins, napkin rings, plates, and stemware, all of which can be interchanged as you see fit

turn the table

IF YOUR TABLE IS ONLY BIG ENOUGH FOR FOUR, HAVE A PIECE OF PLYWOOD CUT TO LARGER DIMENSIONS AT THE HARDWARE STORE AND LAY IT ON THE TOP. A 3- X 6-FOOT RECTANGLE ACCOMMODATES EIGHT PEOPLE.

ring around the candle

NAPKIN RINGS CAN BE TURNED INTO GREAT LITTLE CANDLEHOLDERS FOR TEA LIGHTS. JUST MAKE SURE THE RINGS ARE METAL OR CERAMIC AND NOT FLAMMABLE, AND THAT YOUR TEA LIGHTS ARE THE KIND THAT COME IN THEIR OWN LITTLE TIN CONTAINERS.

THEY'RE A MUST for your entertaining closet: square glass cubes that can be left plain or spray-painted whatever color you choose. Simply arrange them down the center of the table, either symmetrically or asymmetrically, and fill them with a limitless variety of elements. Take a look:

❉ Fill with black polished rocks and a single stalk of curly green bamboo.

❉ Arrange with white orchid blossoms in water for an Asian flair.

For the place settings, we combined matte black dinner plates against wicker chargers topped with celadon salad plates. But feel free to use what you have. Even a simple white everyday plate with a nice green napkin will give a pleasing result. Your everyday stainless flatware never looked better than against a black background, and if you can also tie in napkin rings in stainless—all the better.

❉ Insert live moss and "plant" with a single flower to look as though it's really growing.

❉ For the holidays, fill with pea gravel and paperwhite narcissus bulbs. Or fill containers with miniature Christmas ornaments and weave white lights through the cubes.

❉ An array of dried beans can add great texture. Use sand and cactus to create a southwestern flair.

❉ For kids, try a brightly colored plastic tablecloth (great for those spills) and fill the square containers with multicolored jellybeans. Tie helium-filled balloons to weights and bury them in the jellybeans so they float overhead—wow! A big-time, professional-looking birthday party at minimal expense. Who knew?

crystal blue persuasion

If you look at this finished "formal" tablescape and think *no way can I do that,* remember your guests will probably be saying *"No way did YOU do that!"* And that's the point. You *can* create a memorable party that makes you look like a pro, and it's a lot easier than it looks.

The idea here is to create an elegant, shimmering oasis. By night, it's a candlelit blue lagoon; by day, a cool crystal palace. More importantly, this tablescape is ideal for transitional parties that start, say, at three in the afternoon but don't end until evening (you little party doll, you!). Even better, most of what you have on hand or buy goes back into your cupboard, ready for another use or another party—love that!

A little word of warning here, however: Keep in mind that this is one of those tables that doesn't really come together until the flowers, candles, *and* food are in place.

HERE'S WHAT YOU'LL NEED:

8–10 glass cylinders (These can be vases, glass mixing bowls, soufflé dishes—anything that's clear and reasonably scratch-free. Pyrex containers with writing on them, like beakers and measuring cups, would not work unless you're doing a "high-tech lab" theme—there's an idea!)

Assortment of drinking glasses to invert and support serving dishes (These can be champagne glasses, pilsners, or water glasses. Figure about 4 glasses to support 1 serving dish.)

Glass dinner plates, serving plates, platters, or cake plates—enough to serve whatever is on your menu

Hot glue gun

1 dozen colored tall candles (we chose yellow) and clear candlesticks (optional)

8–10 matching colored votive candles and holders

Several moon lights (battery-operated push-on lights, about $7 each at hardware stores. If you can't find them, just use more votives.)

3–4 yards medium blue to dark blue fabric (the undercloth), or several blue tablecloths

3–4 yards sheer (see-through) blue fabric (We used an iridescent organza.)

A few artificial flower blossoms (hydrangeas, lilies) and blue glass marbles (optional)

2 dozen medium-stemmed flowers (we used yellow calla lilies) and a dozen long-stemmed flowers (we used blue iris)

Crisp, starched dinner napkins

White paper doilies

This is why the accompanying photos show the various stages in building this tablescape—so you know what to expect and don't chicken out. Our version is set up for dessert and cordials, but there are other possibilities. . . .

THIS TABLESCAPE WOULD ALSO BE GREAT FOR:

Tea party or buffet luncheon with finger sandwiches and pick-up food (without candles and moon lights)

Romantic evening buffet (with candles or moon lights)

Cake station for a wedding reception

Baby shower buffet

Anniversary, adult birthday party, or any grown-up occasion where you want to project a more formal attitude without looking pretentious

. . . OR BY THE BOOK:

Pasta, Basta, page 106
Fresh Summer Favorites, page 118
County Fare, page 132

YOU CAN DO IT!

PLACE YOUR BASIC BLUE fabric (or tablecloths) directly on the table to cover it. On top of that layer the iridescent sheer fabric, which you'll later gather and pucker around the lifts and levels to create movement and dimension.

Slide push-on lights between the plain fabric and the iridescent fabric. When on, they'll create a luminous moonlike glow. *Note:* We found these lights needed air circulating around them because of their automatic fire-prevention shut-off gizmos. When we placed one under an inverted cylinder, it shut off and never came back on again—bummer. But under the thin, sheer fabric, they were fine. If you feel at all insecure about using them, omit them and simply add more votives. We even used plain drinking glasses turned upside-down as little stands for the votives, to bring sparkle into the middle of the table.

Now you're ready to begin laying out what goes where. The flowers and candles should be the tallest things on the table, so keep them toward the back. Keep your food lower and closer to the front so it's within easy reach of your guests. Use your imagination and spend the necessary time to lay out your entire table before you begin gluing.

NOW HEAT UP THE GLUE GUN AND FOLLOW ALONG:

- For the cordial station, place an artificial hydrangea under a large, inverted cylinder. Glue a simple glass plate on top. This will support the after-dinner decanter.
- For the tart plate, invert four champagne flutes surrounding a moon light (or votive) and glue a plain glass plate on top. Place a few artificial blossoms on the plate and invert a wide glass bowl over that. Then glue the glass serving plate on top.
- The cupcake pedestal is simply a cheap glass vase left over from a commercial floral arrangement and hot-glued to yet another glass plate.
- One of the flower containers is a smaller cylinder placed inside a larger one, with the gap filled with glass marbles—cool!

You get the idea, right? Follow our photos or your own heart's desire.

STICK WITH ME

THE HOT GLUE GUN should contain the high-temp glue available in craft stores. The hot glue is not used to support the plate's weight but rather to keep it from tipping as guests serve themselves. For that reason, make sure your cylinders or glasses comfortably support each serving piece without wobbling. When the event is over and the glue is dried, it can usually be easily removed without damage. If there's a problem, simply reheat the glue with a blow dryer and peel it away.

A POSY FOR YOUR THOUGHTS

ARRANGEMENTS USING JUST ONE or two kinds of flower always have more impact than fussy multicolored ones—more sophisticated, yet casual too.

BACK ON TOP

WE USED A PLAIN, beat-up banquet table (opposite, top). Who cares—no one will ever see it. If you already have a great table, start from there. We like the fold-up table because it can be stored in the garage when not in use, or, budget permitting, rented. We've also collected our solid and sheer fabrics and a variety of on-hand glass containers to use either as serving pieces or lifts and levels.

Doesn't look like much yet? It will. Here we've determined our lifts and levels, allowing for taller objects—flowers and candles—in back. And just so you can see them, those white round objects are actually battery-operated push-on lights that can be mounted in out-of-the-way places without need for an electrical outlet. How perfect is that for a table in the center of a room? Don't forget to slide them back under the sheer fabric for that moonglow effect. . . .

NOW IT'S TIME FOR THE FUN PART . . .

- Make an uneven row of candles at the back of the table behind the floral containers.
- Create the highest point in the center of the table with long-stemmed iris in mass and yellow artificial blooms (if you like) tucked in around the iris stems. In the other two containers place yellow calla lilies, also in mass.
- For the finishing touches, wrap flatware in crisp white linens and place paper doilies under each dessert.

bountiful country feast

This tablescape proves that several simple center-pieces can be easier to make than one complicated one. Working with natural elements makes table decor easy because there are no mistakes in nature. This concept can be modified for any kind of table, from a traditional dining table to a buffet to a grazing station—you just vary the size and number of pots. Like all of the tablescapes we show you, this one can be a launching point for you to customize as you see fit. We also want to remind you that a small on-hand inventory of basics can have you tablescaping in minutes and with confidence.

WHERE YOU CAN GO WITH THIS:
Casual entertaining with an elegant flair
Thanksgiving
Garden-inspired or outdoor meals
Hearty cook-in or delivered meals
Comfort food, cold-weather-inspired menus

HERE'S WHAT YOU'LL NEED:

Eleven 3-inch terra-cotta pots (from your local garden center)

Four 12-inch white tapered candlesticks

Aluminum foil

Hot glue gun or florist's clay

3 pots live moss (from a garden center or plant shop)

Scissors

Several bunches fresh or dried wispy flowers, such as lavender, heather, or solid aster

2 pounds (approximately) red cherries

20 votive candles in coordinating colors

Thirty-six 4-inch ceramic tiles (from the tile section of the hardware store. We chose shades of mustard, hunter green, and terra-cotta, using 18 for the centerpiece and 3 at each of 6 place settings.)

Solid-colored dinner plates and chargers

Gold Krylon paint stick

6 miniature terra-cotta napkin holders (available at most craft shops)

Solid-colored napkins

Drinking glasses (mix and match)

Everyday flatware

YOU CAN DO IT!

PLACE A DOUBLE ROW of tiles, eighteen total, down the table's center. This defines the area on which to build the centerpiece.

For each of the four candleholders, stand a candle in the middle of a pot and surround it with crumpled aluminum foil until the candle stands upright, leaving about $1\frac{1}{2}$ inches to the top of the pot.

Place four other pots upside down, evenly spaced along the center of the table, atop the tiles. Place a candleholder pot on top of each, secured with hot glue or floral clay.

Remove the moss from the nursery's plastic containers and place in the three remaining pots. Use scissors to poke a deep hole in the center of the moss. Place a bunch of flowers in each hole, trimming them to a height of 6 to 7 inches from the top of the pot. Place them between the candleholder pots.

Fill the candleholder pots with fresh cherries, stem on. How simple is that?

Place individual votives along your ceramic "garden path" to bring light and cheery color down to the surface of the table.

✳ Line a larger terra-cotta pot with a napkin and use it as your breadbasket.

✳ Use an ice-filled pot as a wine cooler. Tie a napkin around the throat of the bottle.

✳ Instead of cherries, try kumquats or limes in a slightly larger pot.

✳ Push three single, brightly colored gerbera daisies into the moss for a splash of color instead of the gold heather effect.

✳ Use three flats of moss from the nursery instead of the tiles. Simply "plant" your candles and flowers directly in the moss.

See how easily this tablescape travels to a buffet? We've filled in with a few more pots of flowers, but otherwise it's the same. Notice how we wrapped our flatware in napkins and stuck it in a pot. Cool, huh?

Place chargers and plates at each place setting.

Place a tile on either side of the plate to support the forks on the left and the spoon and knife at the right.

For placecards, use a gold Krylon paint stick to paint the names of your guests on the remaining tiles. Set them on the plates, on the diagonal.

Thread the napkins through napkin rings and stick a few flowers in each. (If you are unable to find the mini-terra-cotta pots, tie the napkins with raffia or simply fold them into squares and place them on the diagonal under the placecard tiles, letting the napkin corner nearest the edge of the table trail over the edge of the plate, creating a nice double-diamond design.)

veggie-table chic

Take advantage of the produce and flower sections of your grocery superstore. We created five fab centerpieces using only what we found there. Remind yourself that there are no mistakes in nature. Brightly colored fruits and vegetables combined with a few fresh flowers not only make a great statement on the table, they also say a lot about you and your creativity!

THIS WOULD ALSO WORK NICELY FOR:
Easter brunch
Harvest celebration
Separate grazing stations
   throughout the home
Bridal shower

Our color scheme was inspired by a delicious chartreuse silk curtain we turned into a tablecloth. Frances says Scarlett would have been proud. But oops! What's wrong with this picture? While the place-setting police were out, I slipped up and put the napkin on the right. (There I go being dyslexic again. . . .) It goes, of course, to the left of the plate. But you knew that.

HERE'S WHAT YOU'LL NEED:

Here's a list of everything we used—see the instructions for each centerpiece to determine what you'll need for what.

FROM THE PRODUCE DEPARTMENT, WE BROUGHT HOME:

2 large bulbs fresh fennel

2 bunches celery

4 artichokes

I watermelon

4 green apples

I dozen limes

I dozen thin asparagus

2 bags frozen peas

FROM THE FLOWER SECTION, WE PICKED:

I dozen green spider mums

2 small bunches Queen Anne's lace

6–8 yellow gerbera daisies

2 large hydrangea blossoms

6–8 stems white lisianthus

WE HAD AT HOME:

White dinner plates and bowls

Clear glass vases and containers

Floral frogs

Florist's clay

Votive candles

White napkins

Flatware

Wineglasses and goblets

TOP: **Floral frogs are metal, ceramic, or plastic flower holders with perforations or spikes. They can be used alone or set in bowls or vases.**

YOU CAN DO IT!

COVER THE TABLE with chartreuse fabric or a tablecloth.

Set with everyday white dinnerware, simple stemware, and whatever silver or flatware you have.

Using two napkins per guest, turn one on the diagonal at each place setting and let it drape over the edge of the table. This will serve as the placemat. Fold the other napkin on the diagonal and place it to the left of the plate.

Fill clear votive candleholders with yellow or green votives and place them randomly in and around your centerpieces. (See instructions next two pages.)

Use an apple corer to make a hole in the center of a lime at the stem end. Place the lime in a clear votive candleholder and insert a small taper candle into the hole. Place one at each place setting.

Snugly fit a Styrofoam ball into a flowerpot. Stick toothpicks halfway into red and white radishes and stick the other end of the toothpicks into the foam ball. Do three or four of these and place them down the center of the table. Alternate them with taller holders done the same way using fresh Brussels sprouts and cherry tomatoes.

Place celery stalks in glass cylinders and fill them with bunches of baby's breath. Place one of these on each of three flats of sod (from the nursery) and position down the center of the table. With toothpicks, pierce the stems of whole white mushrooms and "plant" them in the grass.

Fill three different-sized glass cylinders with lemons, green apples, and peas. Fill with water. Place small glass plates over the tops and add 2- or 3-inch-diameter round candles. It's a great look that will really last.

Line six teacups and saucers down the center of your table and place a green pear in each cup. Place a short-stemmed flower in a floral vial and press the vial all the way down into the pear so the vial doesn't show. Now put a single orchid stem in the vial. Cluster green grapes on the saucers around each teacup for a chic and simple effect.

who knew?

IN THE EIGHTEENTH CENTURY, THE FANCY FRENCH USED A NAPKIN ONLY ONCE AND THEN TOSSED IT OVER THEIR SHOULDERS. A FOOTMAN INSTANTLY REPLACED IT WITH A FRESH ONE. AT THE END OF THE MEAL THERE WERE PILES OF SOILED NAPKINS BEHIND EACH GUEST'S CHAIR. EEEYEW.

FENNEL FAN

Place the fennel bulb in a large goblet. If it doesn't fit snugly, secure it with a floral frog. Cut several stems of Queen Anne's lace and nestle them into the fine green hair of the fennel—but do it at the last minute so it will last longer.

ASPARAGUS TOPIARY

Use florist's clay to anchor a floral frog in a small bowl. Arrange raw asparagus spears in a circle around the outer edge of the frog. Cut a single hydrangea blossom and place in the center of the frog. The bottom of the blossom should touch the top of the asparagus. Cut fresh limes into thirds and pack them around the asparagus-filled flower frog. Add water. Done!

WATERMELON CENTERPIECE

Cut a small watermelon in half lengthwise and place it in a bowl cut side up. (The bowl should be of a size that will keep the melon half level.) Cut and arrange flowers, sticking them directly in the melon. The water in the melon will keep hearty flowers alive for quite some time! Easy enough?

ARTICHOKE CANDLEHOLDER

Place an artichoke on a small dish and carefully twist a taper candle down into its center. Add spider mums or other hearty blossoms for decoration. That's it!

APPLE PLACECARD HOLDER

You'll need one nice green apple per guest. Make a slit in the top of each apple—just big enough to hold a small placecard. Poke a hole in the apple behind the placecard and insert a single flower in a florist's vial, or fill the hole with water and add the flower directly. The bud should just peek out above the placecard. Place directly on the salad plate or in its own dish on the table. Done!

CELERY STALK FLORAL

Nest a smaller clear container inside a larger one. Pour fresh peas in the space between the two containers. Place a bunch of celery (eight to ten stalks, or whatever fits in your container) in the inner container. Add water. You now have a floral holder to which you may add any flowers you choose. The half-moon centers of the stalks are ideal for keeping your individual flowers straight and tall. Just make sure the flower stems are pushed far enough down to reach the water the celery is sitting in.

tin-talizing picnic

Great ideas sometimes come from the strangest places. At the hardware store the other day we saw all these tin containers in various departments . . . then we looked at each other and said, "Are you thinking what I'm thinking?" Here again, one simple element done in mass provides a great launching point to creativity. And once more, it's about lifts and levels for presenting your food. We set up our picnic on stone steps, but this can just as easily be done on a buffet or a picnic table, or in a shady spot under a tree. Tin tubs, buckets, flowerpots, and good ol' red-and-white checked tablecloths come together to create an informal yet oh-so-clever spread that will have your guests thinking, "Why didn't *I* think of that?" So the next time you're look-ing for inspiration, remember that like elements deliberately arranged can help create fun and easy parties at a moment's notice.

YOU CAN HAVE FUN WITH THIS FOR:

Outdoor picnics

Special holidays like the Fourth of July

Impromptu grilling parties

An indoor winter picnic as an antidote to cabin fever

. . . OR BY THE BOOK:

HERE'S WHAT YOU'LL NEED:

2 red-and-white checked tablecloths

12 matching napkins

Tin buckets, pots, and tubs in assorted shapes
   and sizes

Old newspapers

Serving platters for each food item

Everyday white plates and flatware

DOUBLE YOUR
PLEASURE

When the picnic's over, these useful containers can be
used for their original purposes. We love dual-function,
space-saving elements.

STACKS OF
SUGGESTIONS

* Try stacking white plastic (Tupperware)
  containers with bold-colored napkins. Use with
  white ceramic platters and brightly colored
  gerbera daisies (see Pizza Party, page 63).

* Carry the garden theme a step further with a
  variety of terra-cotta pots, saucers, and containers
  with cut or potted flowers. (See our take on this
  in the Bountiful Country Feast tablescape,
  beginning on page 45.)

* We're cuckoo for kitchen stuff: Haul out the
  stainless-steel pots, pans, and cookie sheets (like
  in our A Night at the Opera table on page 75)
  and use them just as they are for a great kitchen
  gadget tablescape.

GO AHEAD!

Use your imagination! Nothing should be ruled out
when you're planning your party or table decor. What
you might think seems silly could turn out to be just
darn clever!

YOU CAN DO IT!

DRAPE YOUR TABLECLOTHS over whatever surface you'll be using. If
it's a conventional table, simply cover the table with one cloth and
drape the other over a few of the lifts, letting this second cloth cas-
cade and fold beneath and around your serving platters.

Use a large container as a cooler for your beverages and another for
your plates. The latter can be loaded up with the empties and dirties,
and then hauled off to the kitchen when you're done!

Roll the flatware in napkins and place in one of your smaller containers, or simply stick it in willy-nilly, as we've done.

In the containers you'll use for serving food, stuff crumpled newspaper almost to the top. Then scout around for platters and bowls to
fit. These can be anything because they'll never be seen if you cover
them with either lettuce or cloth napkins. How easy is that?

Add color with potted flowers. Plant them in your garden afterward, or, better yet, give them to your guests to take home as favors.

TIN-TALIZING PICNIC **57**

grass roots

This table was created after a trip to our local import store. There we found wooden placecard and napkin holders carved into animal shapes. We thought they'd look great supporting flowers and poking their heads up through wheatgrass. The store also had inexpensive gold trays that would be ideal to contain the wheatgrass. So off to the nursery we went. There we found green papyrus stems and blue iris, which we knew would "heighten" the drama! We were off and running across the savannah—to an evening fit for a Lion King. Clever, exciting, and assembled in under a half-hour!

WHERE YOU CAN GO WITH THIS:
Sit-down dinner where a touch of
 whimsy would be appropriate
Outdoor luncheon or dinner
Exotic Sunday brunch

. . . OR BY THE BOOK:
Brunch for a Bunch, page 92
Al Fresco Feast, page 112
Bollywood Boulevard, page 160

HERE'S WHAT YOU'LL NEED:

1 roll natural-textured paper (from a craft store), or grasscloth

Duct tape

4 flats wheatgrass (or sod), enough to fill 4 gold trays (approximately 11 x 14 inches)

2 dozen papyrus stems

4 thick rubber bands

1 bunch natural raffia

Clear votive candleholders

2 dozen iris

4 pilsner glasses (for flowers)

A few handfuls of polished black pebbles (from craft store)

Four 12- to 16-inch yellow candles

8 animal napkin rings

6 animal placecard holders

6 purple drinking glasses

6 solid colored plates

6 wooden chargers

1 dozen napkins (6 each of two contrasting colors)

6 leather napkin rings

6 jewel-tone votive candles

YOU CAN DO IT!

ROLL THE PAPER LENGTHWISE along the tabletop and secure it underneath at both ends with duct tape.

Fill the four gold trays with wheatgrass or sod.

Bunch together six (or so) papyrus stems and fasten them with a rubber band. Because the stems are thick enough to support themselves and thin enough to be seen around, we stuck the stalks into the grass, tripod style. Then we covered the rubber band with raffia, knotted and clipped.

Invert clear votive candleholders and nestle them into the grass—they'll act as little stands for the animal napkin holders.

Cut the iris stems to equal length, with the blooms just above the rim of the glass. Add pebbles and a single yellow candle. Tie several strands of raffia around each base to visually tie them back into your centerpiece.

Set the table with wooden chargers and solid-colored dinner

❋ If you can't find the textured paper, try using the same matchstick roll-up shade we use in our Bamboozled tablescape on page 67.

❋ Substitute bamboo for papyrus. Bundle several stalks together and top with a Styrofoam ball covered in moss and anchored with florist wire.

❋ Bundle together bear grass or other spiky greenery with a wired floral pick. Insert into a Styrofoam ball. Live potted ivy topiaries can also be used as long as the trunks are tall and don't block the view between guests.

❋ If you can't find small wooden animals, lay a single flower blossom over each napkin. Replace the nesting candleholders with more jewel-tone votives. People will never miss what they never saw.

❋ If you can't find wheatgrass and regular grass is out of season, substitute with moss, black polished pebbles, or a combination of both. Insert individual flowers among the moss and/or stones.

HEY! TRY THIS!

❋ At a separate table, elevate trays onto lifts and levels for a great accompanying grazing station or one-sided buffet.

❋ Use a single tray arrangement on smaller tables, especially if there is more than one table. You might have three tables of six, for example, and two or three grazing stations. This makes for a very cool jungle effect.

plates. The purple drinking glasses are a snazzy touch, but as always, improvise if need be.

Fan-fold together two contrasting napkins and insert them into leather napkin rings or tie them with raffia. Lay them across the dinner plates.

Instead of placecards, clip an iris into each placecard holder. (Do your seating arrangement on a slip of paper and direct your guests when they come to the table.)

Place jewel-tone votives around to bring the flicker of candlelight down to the table's surface.

To keep the table from becoming too fussy, and since it was not a big deal, we omitted the flatware from the setting and instead brought the appropriate utensil with each course. You may do the same or go ahead and set the table as you normally would.

pizza party

What can I say? This is as much fun to make as it is to eat. Oh, wait, someone already said that. . . . Oh well. Once you do this super-easy pizza party, you'll never order in again. (Okay, maybe you will.) But anyway, this one was such a hit that we did it twice, once here in the tablescape section and again in the menu section, page 146. It's even interactive: Guests can pitch in to prepare their own custom pies, since you've so handily prepared all the ingredients in advance and put them within arm's reach.

My inspiration came from these inexpensive metal pie pedestals like you see in old-timey diners. I happened to see

THIS CAN BE A FUN AND UNUSUAL KIND OF:

Birthday party
Stand-up cocktail party
Kids' party
TV/sports party (guys love these pizzas)
Any occasion where you want people to
   have a ball!

OR BY THE BOOK:
Pizza Pizzazz, page 146

HERE'S WHAT YOU'LL NEED:

Mix-and-match table runners, placemats, and napkins

Pizza pedestals (We used a combination of metal diner-style pie pedestals from the restaurant supply place, glass cake plates, pizza pans, and a couple of dinner plates set atop inverted bowls. For other ideas, see Crystal Blue Persuasion, page 39.)

Wooden cutting boards (to add height and texture)

Serving platters for salads and other menu items

Hot glue gun or florist's clay (or other stick 'em clay)

White flowerpots

Potted flowers from the nursery

10 stems of one flower (we used gerberas)

5 stems of a smaller wispy flower (we used freesias)

4 or 5 tall glass cylinder vases

Candlesticks and white candles

White dinner plates

Salad forks

1 pitcher for Sangria or punch

Wine and/or drinking glasses

Small white ramekins and tea lights

Flour

Various shapes of dried pasta

Green apples and pears

White paper doilies

them one day in my local restaurant supply outlet, and I bought several—around $10 apiece. The pie pedestals, combined with cutting boards I already had, plus a little sleight of hand with regular old cereal bowls, drinking glasses, and everyday serving platters, led us to this really snazzy kitchen counter tablescape that looks pretty darn professional, if I do say so myself. Of course it doesn't have to be in the kitchen—it could be anywhere, indoors or out—but having it in the kitchen does give it a relaxed, hang-loose mood that instantly makes your guests feel at home.

glue note
WHEN YOUR HOT-GLUED ITEMS ARE READY TO GO BACK TO THEIR RESPECTIVE CUPBOARDS, THE GLUE IS EASILY REMOVED FROM NONPOROUS SURFACES. IF THE SEAL DOES NOT COME APART IMMEDIATELY, SIMPLY GIVE IT A BLAST WITH YOUR BLOW DRYER, WHICH WILL MELT THE GLUE.

YOU CAN DO IT!

ARRANGE THE RUNNERS AND PLACEMATS on your counter or table-top and then position your various pedestals, cutting boards, and serving platters. You may want to elevate one or more of the cutting boards on inverted bowls or glasses. If so, secure them with a bit of hot glue (see "GLUE NOTE") or florist's clay. Play with the arrangement until it suits you—and you can always change it. Put the higher levels toward the back and the lower ones toward the front. Just make sure all the food will be within easy reach.

Add flowers and water to vases and put potted flowers in white pots. Elevate a pot or two with an inverted pot underneath. This is a lot of look for a little money. Love that.

Line a glass (like we did) or a pot or basket with a napkin and put your forks in it.

Alternate stacking plates with napkins in a sort of spiral pattern.

Set candles in candlesticks and tea lights in small white ramekins. Place them in your tablescape.

For finishing touches, scatter baking flour and dried pasta here and there to augment the theme and texture. Tuck green apples and pears around too. You could also use the kinds of fresh vegetables you associate with pizza: tomatoes, mushrooms, eggplant, onions, artichokes, bunches of herbs, and arugula.

GO TO THE SOURCE

I BUY MOST of my serving platters and dishes at a restaurant supply house. There's one in almost every town. I find the merchandise there costs about half of what it does in specialty stores. And while I do have a magnificent Majolica collection, I find that basic white pottery or porcelain is remarkably versatile. You can dress it up or down, use linens in any color, formalize with fancy charger plates, or mix with flea-market finds. Any way you do it, white and food just look great together.

WE'VE GOTTA HAVE IT

ANOTHER OF MY must-haves is tall glass cylinders for simple flower arrangements. They give a clean, uncluttered look, and you can take 'em anywhere.

LOVE THE ONES YOU'RE WITH

IF YOU DON'T have attractive or matching serving platters, simply line the ones you've got with greens (like kale or romaine lettuce leaves), and no one will know the difference.

bamboozled

Nothing creates drama at the table more than height and scale. This tablescape not only makes a rather grand statement but also illustrates how ordinary beer glasses can be turned into eye-catching centerpieces with a minimum of flowers. It also makes the point that choosing a theme and sticking to it can really pay off. In this case, inexpensive matchstick window shades were our inspiration. A neutral, textured background combined with celadon green and accents of black and gold creates visual balance and a serene, tranquil setting.

YOU'RE A GENIUS SETTING THIS UP FOR:
Sunday brunch
Special romantic occasion
Evening with special friends
Formal dinner
Asian food take-out (Who says
  you have to cook?)

. . . OR BY THE BOOK:
Fresh Summer Favorites, page 118
Bollywood Boulevard, page 160
Fancy-Schmancy, page 166

HERE'S WHAT YOU'LL NEED:

1 matchstick window shade

4 black matchstick placemats

4 pilsner glasses

8 white flowers (we used ranunculus)

12 stems curly bamboo

10 sticks dried bamboo

4 glass plates

2 bags black polished river rock

5 plastic margarita glasses

5 willow balls, or other spheres made from
    woven twigs, available at floral supply shops

5 green taper candles

4 small succulent plants

4 black bowls

8 clear votive candleholders

8 green votive candles

4 gold glass chargers

4 matte black dinner plates

4 celadon salad plates

4 napkins

4 jade stone rings

Bamboo flatware

4 wineglasses

4 water glasses

See how silly it looks before the flowers and willow balls are placed? Do not despair. . . .

YOU CAN DO IT!

REMOVE ALL THE HARDWARE from the matchstick shade and lay the shade lengthwise over the table. Now place the individual placemats on top, letting them drape over the edge of the table.

The centerpieces are simple to assemble. Alternate plastic margarita glasses with pilsners to form a straight line down the center of the table. Place a glass plate under each of the pilsners and fill the plates with polished black rocks.

Divide the flowers and bamboo among the pilsner "vases," keeping the arrangements high and tight so your guests can still see one another.

Place the willow balls on the margarita glasses and insert a long candle through each.

> pssst . . .
> DON'T TELL, BUT THE FLOWERS AND GREEN BAMBOO WE USED ARE ACTUALLY FAKE! THE WATER IN THE GLASS HELPS SELL THE ILLUSION, BUT EVEN OUR PHOTOGRAPHER COULDN'T TELL THE DIFFERENCE. THE BEST PART IS THAT YOU CAN USE THEM OVER AND OVER. EVEN FRESH FLOWERS ARE INEXPENSIVE, AS WE USED ONLY EIGHT STEMS TOTAL.

Transplant the succulents to the black bowls. Their architectural leaves make a chic sculptural statement. You might even like to give them as farewell gifts to your guests.

Now set the table. Start with a gold charger, then a matte black dinner plate, then a celadon salad plate on which you can serve the first course.

Thread your napkins through the jade rings and add glasses and flatware.

And for that final touch of sparkle, distribute the votives randomly among your flowers and candles.

YOU ALWAYS HAVE ALTERNATIVES

* Try inserting candles directly into the succulents or inserting flowers into the willow balls for another great look.

* If the willow balls create too much of a barrier between guests on opposite sides of the table, they can easily be removed to another area during dinner or omitted all together.

* If you don't have bamboo flatware, substitute everyday stainless without regret or hesitation.

* Replace gold charger plates with wicker, blond wood, or silver to tie in with the stainless flatware.

* As with many of our tablescapes, clear glass containers save the day because they are easily integrated into any color scheme. By simply changing the napkins, tablecloth, candles, and flowers, you get a whole new look with the same old ordinary containers. Love that.

* These pilsner centerpieces would also work well on multiple smaller party tables, like for a large reception held in a banquet hall or hotel ballroom. The tall, sculptural arrangements are effective by themselves, but even more so in mass! (There's that term again. . . .)

IT TAKES TWO, BABY . . .

REMEMBER THAT CONFINING your scheme to two dominant colors gives a more dramatic and swank feeling to your table.

Once you've determined the colors and the theme, look for like items to help round it out. You know great tables don't usually just happen by accident; they are deliberate!

fireside chat

To prove that a party can happen anywhere in your home, we created this fireside sit-down for six. We had a sort of *Out of Africa* theme in mind that started with decorative pieces gathered from around the house. The point here is that if you love a certain look that's already a part of your house, try bringing these accessories to the table. In our case, the table was six ottomans pushed together, but your coffee table would work just as well. Serve food that can be eaten with a single utensil and doesn't require cutting.

THIS WOULD BE COZY FOR:
An intimate dinner with close friends
A cold-weather meal to escape the chill
A romantic dinner for two
Hors d'oeuvre and appetizers before dinner
Coffee and dessert after dinner

HERE'S WHAT YOU'LL NEED:

Feel free to substitute your own great accessories for ours!

- 1 faux fur throw
- 6 zebra placemats (from import store)
- 8 zebra-print napkins (6 for guests, 1 for lining breadbasket, and 1 for tying around throat of wine bottle)
- 6 leather napkin rings
- 6 square wooden chargers
- 2 black leather boxes (approximately 12 x 8 x 6 inches)
- 2 decorative wooden boxes (approximately 12 x 6 x 4 inches)
- 1 long trough-like holder or 3 bowls to support 3 honeysuckle twig spheres, to hold 3 short taper candles
- 2 antique wooden candlesticks
- 2 long taper candles
- 2 wooden antique game balls
- 1 crystal wine coaster
- Two 6-inch potted mums (or more— we actually bought a third plant in a coordinating color and cut the flowers to place in a bowl)
- Everyday white dinner plates
- Matte black salad plates
- White soup bowls
- Everyday flatware
- Antique horn
- 1 black flower bowl to hold cut mums

YOU CAN DO IT!

DRAPE THE FAUX FUR throw across the ottomans or table and then set the placemats vertically at each place, using the length to drape down over the ottomans in front of each guest.

Put the wooden chargers down first and then the dinner, salad, and soup dishes. Just pinch the napkins in the center and draw them through the leather napkin rings.

Place the trough or bowls down the center, tuck in three honeysuckle balls, and insert a small taper candle in each.

Add color to the table with potted mums in decorative wooden boxes.

Turn leather boxes into chic breadbaskets and line them with a napkin. (We show two, but one is probably enough.)

Play up the wood-leather look with wooden candlesticks and antique wooden balls.

If you like (and we did), fill an additional ceramic flower bowl with mums snipped from the potted plants.

A-HUNTING WE WILL GO

HUNT AROUND THE HOUSE. If you have a collection of things that look great on your shelves, chances are they'll look just as good on the table. These memento-style centerpieces can be done with almost anything. I've created whimsical tables using lifts and levels to show off the following:

✳ A collection of mismatched teacups and saucers, china compotes, and flea-market picture frames

✳ Vintage and new paper hatboxes

✳ Antique desk and wall clocks

✳ A doll collection

✳ Vintage shoes and handbags lined in plastic and planted with fresh herbs

✳ Sports trophies and related items for a Super Bowl party buffet

✳ Antique toys perched on collectible tin lunchboxes

✳ Costume jewelry draped on miniature papier-mâché dress forms

✳ Mismatched primitive earthenware and pottery

✳ Items with a music theme

✳ You name it. The sky's the limit!

remember . . .

WHAT'S TRUE IN YOUR HOME DECOR ALSO APPLIES TO YOUR TABLE: THINGS GROUPED BY CATEGORY OR BY COLOR ALWAYS LOOK GOOD TOGETHER AND MAKE FOR GREAT CONVERSATION AS WELL. SO FOR THOSE OF YOU WHO THINK YOU CAN'T SET A STUNNING TABLE WITHOUT BUYING EVERYTHING NEW—WAIT! LOOK! AND REDISCOVER THINGS IN YOUR HOME YOU MIGHT HAVE FORGOTTEN—OBJECTS THAT CAN ADD A TOUCH OF SENTIMENT OR CEREMONY TO ANY INTIMATE GATHERING. YOU CAN DO IT!

a night at the opera

This setting illustrates how to combine a buffet service with a seated dinner, but you could easily do the buffet only by stacking the plates on the table or sideboard (or wherever you're serving the buffet). This tablescape began with an old flea-market chandelier we thought would make a great centerpiece. With visions of *Phantom of the Opera* and other stage favorites dancing in our heads, we settled on a mix-and-match jewel-tone color scheme. We needed lifts and levels to create interest and drama. From there we layered fabrics, throws, and shawls for that exotic bohemian flair.

WHERE YOU CAN GO WITH THIS:
An intimate dinner for two to four
Dinner before or after the theater
A holiday buffet
An exotic backyard party

. . . OR BY THE BOOK:
Jambalaya Buffet, page 126
French Country Comfort, page 140
Steakhouse Special, page 154
Bollywood Boulevard, page 160

HERE'S WHAT YOU'LL NEED

. . . FOR THE BUFFET:

Pots and pans of various sizes

3 yards striped fabric

Duct tape or painter's tape

1 silk shawl in a color that goes with your decor

2 chenille throws in coordinating jewel tones

1 flea-market chandelier

1 dozen or so artificial white flowers (we used ranunculus)

2 large tie-back tassels

1 candelabrum

3 mix-and-match silver candlesticks

4 glazed flowerpots

4 heather plants (from the nursery)

1 large bag of chunky orange-colored potpourri

. . . FOR THE TABLE:

4 gold chargers

4 dinner plates (gold, green, and burgundy)

4 ruby wine goblets

4 green stemmed water glasses

4 green silk napkins

4 beaded napkin rings

4 green first-course serving goblets

5 taper candles

8 candle votives

Acrylic flatware

YOU CAN DO IT!

USE DUCT OR PAINTER'S TAPE to wrap the tabletop with striped fabric and secure it underneath. (Afterward, if the duct tape leaves a residue, you can remove it with Goo-Gone.)

On the sideboard or table, position the pots and pans upside down to serve as your lifts and levels. Use as many as you have dishes to serve. (We used four mosaic platters for serving.)

Drape the pots and pans with one or more of your shawls or throws. Now scatter the potpourri over and around. Play with it! Have fun!

Now assemble the individual place settings using what you have or following our list.

ENCORE! ENCORE!

- Take a look around your house and in your closets before you go out to buy anything. An old shawl, scraps of fabric, even covered boxes and small picture frames can be brought to the table to achieve the gypsy-flea-market-theater effect.

- Individual drinking glasses filled with jewel-toned flowers can be added at each place setting for additional splashes of color.

- Small, inexpensive gold tassels can be tied around the napkins and simply laid across the plates. Elegant and simple.

- It's *so* okay to mix silver and gold together as long as you do it evenly around the table—even flatware can be mixed here.

ballroom classics

ENTERTAINING THE MASSES

ow that we've shown you so many tablescapes that are quick and easy and applicable to almost all your home party needs, indulge us as we show you this next section. I have created these designs for clients who paid lots of money for them—but guess what? You don't have to!

Our point is to prove to you that those over-the-top, eye-popping tablescapes you see at big, high-toned events can be truly simple too.

Now before you get crazy, remember they just require a bit more advance planning and ever-so-*basic* crafting. Although they look complicated, they just *aren't*. That's the point. And while they certainly can be done in the home, they also pack a big visual punch in large spaces where you have lots of tables and many guests. If your plan is to impress with lots of drama and little dough, then turn the page. Here are a few of my favorite ballroom classics.

please don't eat the daisies

Hosting a wedding, major banquet, farewell party, or grand event? Don't panic—this one works great for just about any of these affairs. Most of what's on the table (dishes, napkins, glasses, and flatware) is basic stock available at party rental places. The centerpieces and what's overhead you can make yourself. They may look like a million bucks—but they don't cost it.

WOULD BE BLOOMIN' FESTIVE FOR:

Multiple tables where transforming a banquet hall, ballroom, or other large space could be costly

Large events where you rent the basics but don't want or need to hire a professional florist

Where you need a dramatic design element that can instantly theme your event but is also easily transportable and can be set up within an hour

. . . OR BY THE BOOK:

Steakhouse Special, page 154

Fancy-Schmancy, page 166

OOPS—We did it again—put the napkin on the right. We know you know better. What were we thinking?

HERE'S WHAT YOU'LL NEED PER TABLE:

Twelve 6-inch Styrofoam balls (9 for hanging and 3 for the table, available at craft shops)

12 to 14 artificial daisy blossoms per ball (or enough to cover), plus one daisy for each napkin ring

Hot glue gun

Several spools of thin curling ribbon

12- or 14-inch upholstery needle

Thumbtacks

Daisies to tie around each napkin at each place setting

Votive candles and holders, allowing one or more per guest

Optional: Wooden letters from craft stores for each of your guest's initials, spray-painted silver

Rentals: linens, dishes, glasses, flatware (Or bring your own, but renting is probably cheaper in this case.)

YOU CAN DO IT!

PLUG IN YOUR GLUE GUN and set it aside. With a wire cutter or clippers, cut the daisies, leaving about an inch of the plastic stem to poke into the Styrofoam balls. Reinforce with a touch of hot glue as you place each stem in the ball.

Repeat until the ball is covered. Don't be stingy.

When three identical balls are finished, thread the upholstery needle with thin ribbon. Measure enough ribbon to have about 3 inches between balls, with the bottom ball 24 to 30 inches from the table. Knot the ribbon at the bottom of each ball. Attach the top of the ribbon to the ceiling with a thumbtack, letting the three-ball daisy chain hang down. Repeat with the remaining two chains.

Place the remaining three balls directly on the table or propped up slightly on a little clear glass bowl or empty votive holder.

Fold white napkins into thirds lengthwise and place them so they drape down off the table.

Cut as many more daisies as there are napkins, leaving 6 to 8 inches of stem and a few of the green leaves. Twist these around each napkin and insert the silverware, as we did, or place the daisies alongside the plates.

For a personalized touch, and if budget and time permit, place silver-spray-painted wooden letters in each guest's initials at his or her place. These also make nice take-home party mementos.

Add votive candles and voilà!

perennial party props
WHEN THE EVENT IS FINISHED, YOU CAN STORE ALL THE DAISY BALLS IN PLASTIC BAGS TO BE USED AGAIN AND AGAIN!

safety first
IF YOUR BANQUET HALL SAYS, AND MOST DO, THAT EVERYTHING YOU BRING IN MUST BE FLAME RETARDANT, YOU CAN BUY FLAME-RETARDANT SPRAY IN THE HARDWARE STORE. IT'S COLORLESS, SO IT WON'T HURT YOUR DESIGNS.

TIMING TIPS

With the help of a few friends you can assembly-line this process and do the entire room in an evening. If it's just you, you'll need about fifteen minutes to assemble each ball, so calculate your time accordingly.

IT'S NOT NICE TO FOOL MOTHER NATURE —TOO MUCH . . .

Whatever flower you choose, make sure that real flowers actually grow in that color and that all the blossoms are the same. Otherwise it will look too fake. White goes with anything, but colors can be very effective. Look ahead to page 85 for our red and orange rose extravaganza!

BLOOMING WITH IDEAS

- Hot-glue daisies onto inexpensive napkin rings to use for any occasion.

- Try white artificial roses and dried baby's breath for a delicate and romantic touch.

- As placecards, try small picture frames with a daisy hot-glued to each one. Write the names in each frame or—even better—insert the guest's photo.

- You can eliminate the balls on the table and instead do vases of live daisies. That way they'll really never know what's real and what's not! The price is about the same.

- To add height to the table, you can substitute medium-sized taper candles for votives. Just make sure they clear the hanging flower balls.

everything's coming up roses

Now let's take this "entertaining the masses" bit one step further. Before you pooh-pooh the idea of doing your own flowers for a large event, remember that height, color, and volume are what make a really special statement. In the last chapter, you saw how Styrofoam and artificial flowers created a big, extravagant look. This chapter takes that same skill and idea into a more conventional realm where, again, multiple tables come into play. But conventional doesn't mean boring. Take a look at this incredible tablescape.

Here, a rose topiary surrounded by candle arrangements shows how height and color can really zip up a humdrum scheme. Whether you stage this in a ballroom or your own living room for a special event, this idea is simple and stunning.

WOULD BE IMPRESSIVE FOR:

A charity luncheon

A wedding, at home or in a ballroom

An anniversary dinner

Any formal special occasion

. . . OR BY THE BOOK:

Lunch on the Sundeck (for the menu, not the location!),
  page 98

Steakhouse Special, page 154

Fancy-Schmancy, page 166

HERE'S WHAT YOU'LL NEED PER TABLE:

IF USING FRESH ROSES:

Four 4-inch half-spheres of water-soaked Oasis
(floral foam)

One 6-inch full sphere of water-soaked Oasis
(Note: You may have to piece together a
6-inch sphere using floral tape. You could also
mold a piece of chicken wire around a 4-inch
cube and just make sure you leave the stems
long enough to reach through the wire
sphere to the Oasis.)

IF USING ARTIFICIAL ROSES:

Four 4-inch half-spheres Styrofoam

One 6-inch sphere Styrofoam

6 dozen peach, coral, and red roses, 24 for tall
topiaries and 48 for 4 half-spheres

24-inch-tall candlesticks (used to make
topiaries; see Rentals list)

One 3-inch length of ¾-inch-wide dowel rod

Florist's clay

4 peach-colored taper candles

4 coral-colored starched napkins

1 can gold spray paint

4 curtain finials

Placecards

---

rent-a-tip
SOME RENTAL COMPANIES HAVE
CHAIRS WITH SEATS OR SEAT
COVERS THAT CAN BE ORDERED
TO MATCH YOUR LINENS, SO
ASK ABOUT THEM.

don't rent-a-tip
BIG DISCOUNT AND ODD-LOT
STORES SELL BASIC DINNER
PLATES FOR CHEAP. SO DO
RESTAURANT SUPPLY STORES. IF
THERE'S ONE NEAR YOU, KEEP
AN EYE OUT. IT COULD BE
CHEAPER THAN RENTING, AND
YOU OWN THEM.

RENTALS:

Tables

Chairs

Tablecloths

Water glasses

Wine and/or champagne
  glasses

Dinner plates

Salad plates

Bread and butter plates

Flatware

24-inch candlesticks, in real
  brass or silver or
  painted to look it,
  1 per table

RIGHT: Here we see what most
ordinary events look like. Nice
table, demure little centerpiece,
expensive! By doing it yourself
with a bit of flair, you get lots of
drama for much less money.

YOU CAN DO IT!

IN THE TALL CANDLESTICK, in the hole where the candle would normally go, insert the dowel piece and anchor it with florist's clay. This will be the spike for your finished floral sphere.

Cutting at an angle, snip the rose stems about 2 inches long and insert them into your water-soaked Oasis or dry Styrofoam. Cover the foam completely.

Place the sphere atop the dowel spike in the candlestick.

Put the half-spheres on small plates and push a tall candle into each one. Place them around the base of the topiary.

With gold spray paint, paint the wooden finials. With a coping saw, make a small slit in the top of each and insert your placecards, or just prop the cards against the finials.

Roll the napkins and stand one upright in each guest's wine or champagne glass.

. . . REAL AND ARTIFICIAL FLOWERS. To help stretch the budget, we used fake flowers for the tall topiary spheres and the real thing for the half-spheres on the tables. People are more inclined to touch the candleholders in front of them, and the fragrance is simply another bonus.

FLOWER POWER

If you use fresh flowers, make sure the buds are tight when you buy them, and then soak your Oasis in warm water with a few tablets of aspirin. This will help open the buds and keep the leaves from falling or wilting. You can assemble the spheres the night before the event, spritz them with water, place them in a plastic bag, blow air into the bag, and tie. When using artificial buds, make them as far in advance as you like, but cover them so they stay dust free.

CARRY ON!

✳ Try using the white daisies from the last chapter for an all-white effect. White roses are ideal for weddings.

✳ Before the guests arrive, spray the room with rose-scented spray or spritz your flowers with rosewater, available in most craft and bed and bath shops.

✳ Scatter real rose petals around the table to help sell the illusion that all your flowers are real.

✳ For a festive look, try multicolored gerbera daisies (real and/or fake) with different primary-color napkins. Make placecard holders out of tiny Styrofoam balls covered with jelly beans.

✳ To economize, make two candle arrangements instead of four. Fill in with votives.

brunch for a bunch

lunch on the sundeck

pasta, basta

al fresco feast

fresh summer favorites

jambalaya buffet

county fare

french country comfort

pizza pizzazz

steakhouse special

bollywood boulevard

fancy-schmancy

ridiculously easy recipes

12 GREAT MENUS

NOW BEFORE YOU PLEAD THE FIFTH on cooking, take a deep breath. The following recipes are not only tried and true, they are intentionally super simple. They have been professionally tested not only for flavor but for ease of preparation. And they serve up beautifully. While many of these dishes are healthy, some are totally indulgent. So sue me. I'll say it again—your dinner party is no place for a nutrition clinic. People are there to have a good time and to break their diets, not start them! Try a few dishes on friends and family, too. Nothing will boost your confidence more than "I can't believe how good this is and that you made it!"

The menus were designed with lead time in mind. We've even broken down the steps of preparation to make sure you stay on schedule and out of overwhelm. Many of the menus can be made well in advance and require more assembly than actual cooking—but they look so impressive that no one will ever know you cheated (hee-hee) with cans, bags, and boxes of prepared foods. Just promise me you'll ditch the commercial cartons and keep our little secrets, wouldja?

Although we've given you our suggested menus, many of the individual dishes can be mixed and matched as your taste desires. In many cases we've even given you substitutions to prove just how flexible these dishes are. Our divine food tester, Laurie Woolever, wanted to be sure we stressed that these recipes are great bases to serve as they are or to spice up as you see fit. Most of them can be easily adapted to feed from six people to a crowd and can be served sit-down or buffet style.

In our tablescaping section we suggest menus that work with specific events, so you just can't make a mistake.

And lastly, put yourself in a positive frame of mind. It's a wonderful feeling to open your door with confidence and watch people having a great time in your home. If you cook with your heart and not your ego, your get-together will be a loving experience for everybody.

P.S.: The big cold box is the refrigerator; the hot box is the oven; and the hot surface is the stovetop.

Just in case you were wondering. . . .

Brunch for a Bunch

Cinnamon-Pecan Sticky Buns

———

Oranges and Cantaloupe

———

Egg-Chili-Cheese Bake

———

Spicy Link Sausages

WINE/BEVERAGE SUGGESTION: CHAMPAGNE, SPARKLING WINE, MIMOSAS

IF YOUR bunch is bigger than the six to eight these recipes serve, you can easily double them. While this is billed as a brunch, it would work just as well as a lunch or casual dinner, in which case I'd add a green salad with avocado and do the sticky buns or fruit for dessert. (Warm the sticky buns and serve with vanilla ice cream!) In any case, the only thing you make is the casserole, which can be prepared in advance. I swear it is just as good the next day out of the fridge as it is fresh from the oven. Buy brown-and-serve sausages, kielbasa, or turkey sausage, or go for authentic spicy Mexican chorizo. You could also have ham or bacon, of course. You shouldn't have any trouble finding volunteers to research the best sticky buns you can buy, whether from your local bakery or from the supermarket—or you can bake our version of homemade. Speaking of bread, you may want to serve a neutral bread with the meal. If so, we'd suggest stacks of buttered white or whole wheat toast, served in a napkin-lined basket.

HOW TO DO IT:

* Prepare all ingredients for the casserole, so all you need to do is assemble and bake it. About an hour before your guests arrive, preheat the oven and assemble the casserole. Put it in the oven about an hour before you want to eat.

* If you are going with our "homemade" version of the sticky buns, make them ahead and re-heat. If purchasing, wrap them in foil so they are ready to be warmed in the oven. If you make or purchase more than a day in advance, freeze rather than refrigerate them. Bread gets rubbery in the fridge.

* If the sausages need to be cooked, do this in advance and then refrigerate them.

* Cut up the fruit and arrange it on a platter. Cover it with cling wrap and put it in the fridge.

* Prepare your beverages and bar. Are you serving juice? Bloody Marys? Screwdrivers? Get out pitchers, and cut up lemons or limes and refrigerate. Put out glasses, spoons, ice bucket, cocktail napkins, etc.

* That morning, if it's breakfast or brunch, set out coffee in a thermos, cream and sugar, and cups or mugs on the table or kitchen counter (but out of your way), so guests may help themselves.

* Warm the buns or pastries to put out with the coffee. You could also put out the tray of fruit for guests to nibble.

* Warm the sausages in the microwave, oven, or skillet before serving, but they do not have to be piping hot.

cinnamon-pecan sticky buns

PREP:

8- or 9-inch round cake pan

---

4 tablespoons (¹/₂ stick) butter, melted

¹/₂ cup brown sugar, lightly packed

²/₃ cup pecans, coarsely chopped

I cylinder package refrigerated cinnamon rolls, such as Pillsbury (toss the icing packet)

SERVES 6 TO 8
PREP TIME: 15 MINUTES
BAKING TIME: 20 TO 25 MINUTES

Use store-bought or the following fake-it-don't-make-it version, which can easily be doubled.

❋ Preheat oven to 375°F.

❋ Pour the melted butter into the cake pan. Rub a little on the sides of the pan so the rolls don't stick.

❋ Sprinkle the brown sugar and pecans around the bottom of the pan. Place the uncooked rolls on top.

❋ Bake 20 to 25 minutes.

❋ Place a plate over the top of the pan and then invert to turn the rolls onto the plate. Watch wonderful gooey caramel oozing everywhere.

oranges and cantaloupe

SERVES 6 TO 8

PREP TIME: 15 MINUTES

Judge a cantaloupe by its smell. If it smells like a ripe, juicy cantaloupe, then it is one. If it doesn't, it isn't. Also there should be a slight springiness to touch at the stem end.

✳ Here's the easiest way to deal with a cantaloupe: Cut the cantaloupe in half crosswise and scoop out the seeds. Cut the halves into four wedges each and then cut off the rind. Peel and section the oranges if you like, cutting away the white pith and membranes. If you don't like, just cut the oranges into sections and call it a day. If you want to be creative with your presentation (of course you do!), you can cut the oranges into round slices instead of wedges and mound them in the center of a round platter. Surround with the cantaloupe wedges overlapping, like petals. Garnish with berries, sprigs of fresh mint, pansies, or nasturtiums.

---

i propose a toast...

IF YOU'RE PREPARING TOAST FOR A CROWD, HEAT THE OVEN TO 350°F AND LINE A COOKIE SHEET WITH BREAD SLICES. TOAST 3 TO 5 MINUTES ON EACH SIDE, DEPENDING ON YOUR OVEN AND YOUR PREFERENCE. THEN RUB THE HOT SURFACE WITH THE SMALL END OF A STICK OF BUTTER, OR USE A PASTRY BRUSH TO PAINT IT WITH OLIVE OIL—WHICH IS YUMMY.

---

1 ripe cantaloupe

3 large navel oranges

egg-chili-cheese bake

SERVES 6 TO 8
PREP TIME: 15 MINUTES
BAKING TIME: 50 TO 60 MINUTES

As I said earlier, this is easy to prepare ahead and then to assemble and bake à la minute. But you could certainly do ahead completely and reheat if you wanted.

* Preheat the oven to 350°F. Rub butter or nonstick spray along the sides and bottom of your baking dish.

* Combine the eggs, corn, chiles, salsa, cheeses, Worcestershire sauce, and cornmeal. Season with salt and red or black pepper, and mix well. Bake 50 to 60 minutes, until lightly browned and set—that is, the middle isn't wobbly.

TIP

A ¹/₂-pound (8-ounce) block of cheese makes 2 cups of grated cheese. Of course you can use packaged, pregrated cheese (we like Sargento). It doesn't have quite as much flavor as freshly grated, but it'll do in a pinch.

PREP:

For one recipe, use a 1¹/₂ quart casserole. If doubling the recipe, use a 9 × 13-inch baking dish.

Butter or nonstick spray

8 large eggs, beaten

One 17-ounce can cream-style corn

Two 4.5-ounce cans green chiles

¹/₃ cup salsa, such as Paul Newman's medium spicy, plus extra for serving on the side

1¹/₂ cups shredded Monterey Jack cheese

1¹/₂ cups shredded extra-sharp Cheddar cheese

2 teaspoons Worcestershire sauce

2 tablespoons cornmeal or grits

Salt and red or black pepper, to taste

Sour cream, if desired

Chopped parsley to garnish, if desired

spicy link sausages

COOKING TIME: 5 TO 7 MINUTES FOR PRECOOKED SAUSAGE;
ABOUT 20 FOR FRESH SAUSAGE

The brown-and-serve variety is the easiest, but it really isn't that much more trouble to get good-quality sausage from the butcher, or better yet, from one of those good eco-friendly farming outfits like Niman Ranch, which you can find on the Internet. You could also have kielbasa, turkey or chicken sausage, or authentic Mexican chorizo, which is hot hot hot. Brown or fry according to package or your butcher's instructions. Keep covered in foil in a warm (250°F) oven until serving.

TIP

To cook fresh sausage, place a skillet over medium-high heat and bring about ¹/₂ inch of water to a simmer. Pierce the sausages with a fork so the skins do not burst. Put the sausages in the water, cover, and cook 8 to 10 minutes. (Test one by cutting it; it should have lost its pinkness.) Pour off the liquid and return the skillet to heat, shaking the sausages around so they brown evenly.

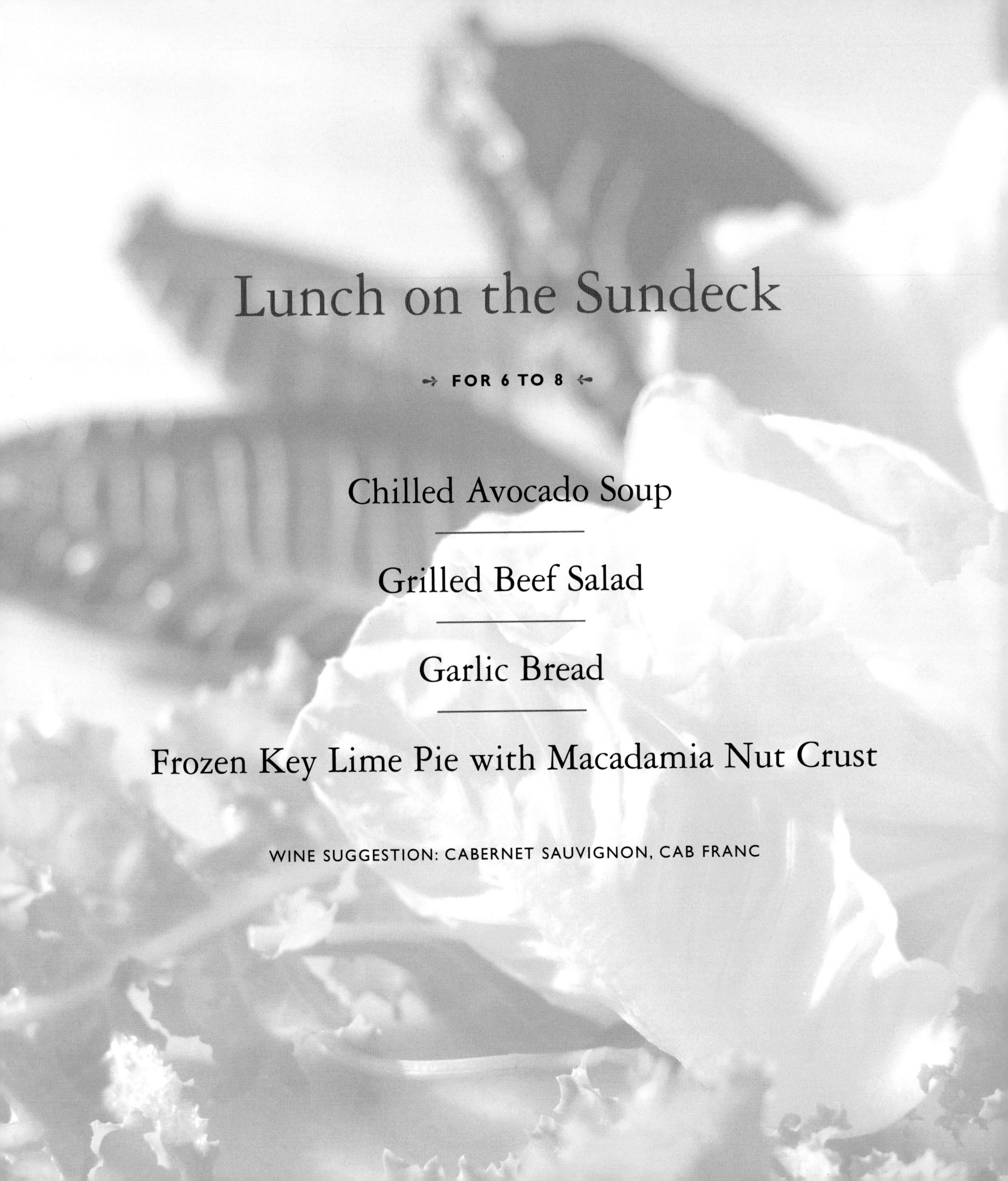

Lunch on the Sundeck

→ **FOR 6 TO 8** ←

Chilled Avocado Soup

Grilled Beef Salad

Garlic Bread

Frozen Key Lime Pie with Macadamia Nut Crust

WINE SUGGESTION: CABERNET SAUVIGNON, CAB FRANC

THIS IS ONE of my favorites and men really like it because it's STEAK, you know? The whole shebang can be made entirely in advance, and it's economical, too. The only last-minute thing is to heat the bread, and judging from the leftovers (zero), even the bread is good at room temperature. So you can completely relax with this one.

INSTANT HORS D'OEUVRE
Gourmet and specialty foods shops are great sources for a packaged, simple, but satisfying hors d'oeuvre. We suggest cheese straws or cheese wafers with this menu, but any savory nibble will do.

BREADWINNER
The foil-wrapped garlic bread in the frozen foods section at the grocery store is usually pretty darn good.

HOW TO:

Like we said, this can all be made in advance. The pie you can do a week in advance; the soup, three days; the salad, the day before or morning of.

All that's left before the party is setting the table and the bar with all the plates, glasses, flatware, and serving pieces.

Serve the soup family style at the table or in individual bowls from the kitchen.

Put the bread in the oven to warm, following package instructions. Serve it in a basket lined with a cloth or napkin.

Take the salad out 30 minutes to an hour before serving, and line your plates with lettuce leaves. Just before you sit down to the soup, spoon the beef salad onto the plates. Garnish with a bit of parsley, if you like.

Take the pie out of the refrigerator just before you sit down to the main course. If you're doing the extra bit with whipped cream and toasted coconut, whip the cream while you let your guests clear the table. (You know how they're always asking if they can help . . . let 'em!)

chilled avocado soup

PREP:

Food processor

THE SOUP:

2 large avocados, peeled and pitted

Two 10½-ounce cans chicken broth

Juice of 1 lime (about 2 tablespoons)

1 teaspoon ground coriander

1 teaspoon ground cumin

Salt and black pepper, to taste

THE (OPTIONAL) GARNISH:

½ cup prepared salsa

½ cup sour cream

Chopped cilantro

SERVES 6 TO 8
PREP TIME: 15 MINUTES

So simple, and with a wonderful velvety texture. The salsa and sour cream garnish gives it just the right little kick, but it's fine without. For that matter, if you're in a last-minute mode, you could make this with nothing but avocado and chicken broth. Love that.

❋ Place the peeled avocado, chicken broth, lime juice, spices, and salt and pepper in a blender or food processor and purée until smooth. Taste and add more salt and pepper if necessary. Chill.

❋ To serve, pour the soup into cups or bowls. If you like, plop a bit of salsa and sour cream on top and sprinkle with chopped cilantro.

LEFTOVERS?
The avocado soup is good as a dip for toasted tortillas or as a condiment for a burrito or wrap.

TIP

If you want to juice a lemon or lime, put it in the microwave for 40 to 60 seconds first. It will be bursting with juice!

grilled beef salad

Cutting board and knife
Large bowl to hold salad

1½ pounds boneless sirloin or tenderloin, about 1 inch thick

Salt and black pepper, to taste

1 tablespoon butter

One 15-ounce can new potatoes, drained

One 15-ounce can hearts of palm, drained and chopped diagonally in 1-inch pieces

One 8-ounce jar roasted red peppers, drained and coarsely chopped

1 small red onion, thinly sliced into rings

1 cup cherry or grape tomatoes

1 head romaine or leaf lettuce, or a combination

TIP

Hot enough for ya?
The skillet is hot enough when you touch a corner of the meat to the pan, and it sizzles.

SERVES 8
PREP TIME: 20 MINUTES
COOKING TIME: 7 TO 10 MINUTES

This is a good recipe to ad-lib, improvise, whatever. The key components are the beef and the dressing, but after that, add or subtract ingredients as you like, or use what you have on hand. This dish is also a good use for leftover steak.

✳ Rub the beef on both sides with salt and pepper. Place a stovetop grill pan or heavy skillet on medium-high heat and add the butter. For a 1-inch-thick steak, medium rare, cook about 5 minutes on one side and 3 minutes on the other. Let the beef cool while you prepare the remaining ingredients. *Note:* If you like your beef rare, you might want to undercook it a bit, as the vinegar in the dressing "cooks" it a little more.

✳ Prepare the Vinaigrette Dressing (recipe follows), or use bottled dressing (see Note).

✳ In a large bowl, place the drained potatoes, hearts of palm, peppers, sliced onion, and tomatoes. (If using cherry tomatoes, you may want to slice them in half lengthwise.)

✳ Slice the beef into thin strips, about ¼ to ½ inch wide and about 2 inches long. Add the beef to the bowl.

✳ Pour the vinaigrette over all and refrigerate. (Take the salad out of the fridge 30 minutes before serving; you don't want it ice cold.)

✳ To serve, line a large serving bowl or individual plates or bowls with lettuce leaves and mound the salad on top. Season with salt and freshly ground pepper.

NOTE
Foods served cold do not release their flavors as fully as warm foods. So what's the moral here? Cold foods need more seasoning—and they may benefit from sitting at room temperature for a while, as long as there is no danger of spoiling.

vinaigrette dressing

PREP TIME: 5 MINUTES

This is a classic vinaigrette and really tastes so much better than the store-bought varieties that it's worth the five minutes it takes to make. Great for a simple salad or to marinate fresh veggies.

Note: When serving Grilled Beef Salad, you may want to "beef up" your dressing as well with an extra teaspoon of mustard, another tablespoon of lemon or lime juice, or another dose of salt before serving.

PREP: I find it easiest to make this in a jar with a screw-on lid, but you can whisk it in a bowl or whir it in a blender if you like.

1/4 cup white or red wine vinegar
1 teaspoon Dijon mustard
1 teaspoon chopped garlic
1/2 teaspoon salt
1/2 teaspoon pepper
3/4 cup olive oil

✳ In a jar or small bowl, combine the vinegar, mustard, garlic, salt, and pepper. Add the olive oil, tighten the lid, and shake like crazy—or whisk in the olive oil until emulsified—or whir it all in the blender.

"DRESSING UP"

If you like your dressing a bit spicier, add a pinch of red pepper flakes or a dash of hot sauce to the vinaigrette. For an Asian flavor, try rice wine vinegar in place of regular wine vinegar, or sesame oil in place of olive oil. A teaspoon or two of soy sauce instead of salt is good, too. Chopped fresh or dried mint gives a hint of fresh sweetness.

frozen key lime pie with macadamia nut crust

MAKES ONE 10-INCH PIE
PREP TIME: 40 MINUTES
FREEZING TIME BEFORE SERVING: 2 HOURS

PREP:

Microplane or regular grater for grating citrus zest
10-inch deep-dish pie plate
Food processor, for making crust

THE CRUST:

1 cup shredded coconut

1 cup macadamia nuts (about 4¹/₂ ounces)

¹/₄ cup (¹/₂ stick) butter, softened

20 vanilla wafers

2 tablespoons flour

THE FILLING:

¹/₂ cup fresh lime juice (about 6 limes' worth)

Grated zest of 2 limes

One 14-ounce can sweetened condensed milk

2 cups whipped topping, such as Cool Whip

TIP

These new microplane graters are amazing. Find them at hardware or kitchen supply stores.

The crust makes this special, but the filling ain't all bad either. Point being, if you want to use a ready-made graham cracker crust, you know you have my blessing. And if you want to cut a few calories, use the nonfat condensed milk; it's fine in this recipe.

* Heat the oven to 375°F, and check the TIP on page 100.

* In a large dry skillet on medium heat, stir the coconut until it turns golden brown, 3 to 4 minutes.

* Put ³/₄ cup of the coconut, the nuts, butter, vanilla wafers, and flour into a food processor and process until the consistency of very coarse crumbs. Save the remaining ¹/₄ cup coconut for topping.

* Pat the crumb mixture into the bottom and sides of a 10-inch deep-dish pie plate and bake 15 minutes. The crust needs to cool completely, so you may want to put it in the fridge, uncovered, while you make the filling.

* Mix all the filling ingredients together and spoon the mixture into the cooled crust.

* Sprinkle with the reserved ¹/₄ cup toasted coconut.

* Freeze at least 2 hours before serving.

EXTRA

Instead of topping the pie with coconut, leave it bare and freeze. Then, to serve, remove the pie from the freezer and top with real whipped cream in pretty peaks and swirls. *Then* sprinkle with the toasted coconut and decorate with thin, twisted slices of lime. How to whip cream just right? See page 124.

Pasta, Basta

FOR 6 TO 8

Crostini with Olive Tapenade

Green Salad with Warm Goat Cheese
and Toasted Pine Nuts

Linguini with Tuna, White Beans, and Tomatoes

Lemon Sherbet with Gingersnaps

WINE SUGGESTION: PINOT GRIGIO

I N ITALIAN, "pasta, basta" means "pasta, enough," and it is. This combination of flavors is so satisfying you won't want another thing—but a green salad with a little goat cheese would be nice. This is a great last-minute out-of-the-pantry party and makes a wonderful weekend lunch.

HOW TO DO IT:

* You can easily make the pasta the night before, or the morning of, but it's also no problem at the last minute—all it takes is the time to open a few cans and boil water—so go ahead and do that and get it out of the way. Cover and refrigerate if you prepare the pasta more than an hour before serving.

* Set out the tapenade and crostini, breadsticks, whatever.

* Prepare the goat cheese and pine nuts for the salad.

* Set the table, chill the wine, and get out the dessert bowls or plates, and that's about it. Plunk down the salad and pasta on the table together, *basta.* Pour the wine and while away the day.

crostini with olive tapenade

SERVES SIX TO EIGHT
PREP TIME: 5 TO 10 MINUTES

One 8-ounce jar tapenade

One or two baguettes (depending on size) or one 16-ounce package breadsticks

* Ready-made all the way. The "crostini" can be plain pita or bagel chips, crackers, or bread sticks. If you want to be more authentic, toast thin slices of Italian or French bread, and while they're still warm, rub one side with a half clove of garlic. Olive tapenade is nothing more than olives ground up with a little olive oil and garlic. If you find it too salty, mix in a few tablespoons of fresh basil and/or parsley that have been whizzed in the food processor. To serve, spoon the tapenade into a little bowl and arrange the crostini around it.

green salad with warm goat cheese and toasted pine nuts

6–8 cups loosely packed salad greens, depending on the number of guests and their appetites

3–4 tablespoons pine nuts

1 egg

1 cup bread crumbs

4 tablespoons butter or olive oil (or combination of both)

12–16 ounces (2 logs) goat cheese, cut in ¾-inch-thick round slices

Vinaigrette Dressing (page 103 or store-bought)

SERVES 6 TO 8
PREP TIME: 20 MINUTES, 10 IF YOU DON'T WARM THE CHEESE

Do I need to tell you to use those wonderful bags of prewashed salad greens? Didn't think so. And if you want to skip the "warm" part of the goat cheese, just crumble the cold cheese on the salad and sprinkle with the pine nuts. If you are going to sauté the cheese as follows, make sure it is good and chilled beforehand so it slices easily.

* Place the greens on individual salad plates and set aside.

* Put the pine nuts in a dry medium skillet on medium heat. Shake and stir until pale golden, about 3 to 4 minutes. Or you may toast them in a 350°F oven for 3 to 4 minutes. Either way, set the timer so you don't forget them; they continue to cook once you remove them from the heat, and they burn easily. Set aside.

* In a small bowl, beat the egg with 1 tablespoon water. Put the bread crumbs in a small bowl or on a sheet of wax paper. Put the skillet used for the pine nuts on medium-high heat and add 2 tablespoons butter and/or olive oil.

* Dip the cheese rounds in the egg mixture and then roll them in the bread crumbs. Put half of them in the pan and sauté until golden brown, a minute or two on each side, and remove. Add the remaining 2 tablespoons butter and/or oil, let it heat, and sauté the remaining goat cheese rounds. Set aside.

* Drizzle the salad greens with vinaigrette, top with a round or two of warm goat cheese, and sprinkle with the toasted pine nuts. Voilà!

linguini with tuna, white beans, and tomatoes

Two 5-ounce cans tuna

One 15-ounce can white beans (kidney, cannellini, or Great Northern), rinsed and drained

One 15-ounce can diced tomatoes

1 teaspoon chopped garlic

1/2 cup olive oil

1/4 cup lemon juice

1/4 cup chopped fresh basil (optional)

1 pound regular or whole wheat linguini

Salt and black pepper to taste

1/4 cup chopped fresh parsley (optional)

SERVES 6 TO 8

PREP TIME: 20 MINUTES

You know how you just want to taste something and 5 minutes later you've eaten the whole thing? This is one of those things, so watch out. Best served warm or at room temp. Can easily be made ahead and refrigerated, but take the dish out 30 minutes or so before serving. If you do make it ahead, you may want to drizzle it with a little more olive oil before serving, as the pasta will soak it up as it sits. Taste first. Speaking of taste, we find the oil-packed tuna more flavorful and better suited to this dish than the water-packed variety, but if you're counting calories, we understand. If you like tomatoes or want a little more color, by all means add another cup or so of tomatoes.

✳ Put a large pot of water on to boil. Covering it makes it boil more quickly. Meanwhile . . .

✳ In a large bowl, combine the tuna, beans, tomatoes, garlic, olive oil, lemon juice, and basil (if you have it).

✳ Add a tablespoon or so of salt to the boiling water and cook the pasta according to package instructions. Drain and add to the tuna mixture, tossing well.

✳ Season with lots of salt and pepper, sprinkle with parsley, and serve.

PASTA POINTER

You want to cook pasta al dente, or "to the tooth," which is to say firm to the tooth, but not crunchy. Taste for doneness as you go. Don't overcook; you don't want it mushy, either.

VARIATION

For a change, or if someone doesn't like tuna, we think canned clams, baby shrimp, or salmon (all rinsed and drained) are a nice substitute.

lemon sherbet with gingersnaps

1 QUART ICE CREAM SERVES 4 TO 6
(BETTER HAVE 2 QUARTS!)
PREP TIME: 10 MINUTES

Lemon and ginger are a great flavor combination. Find a premium-brand lemon sherbet or sorbet, like Haägen-Dazs, and plain old store-bought gingersnaps. Scoop the sherbet or sorbet into bowls and place a few cookies in or around, or pass the cookies separately. Or, if you want to gussy it up a little, here are a few suggestions:

- Soften the sherbet in the microwave for 30 seconds and fold in strips of fresh mint, then allow to refreeze before serving.
- Soften the sherbet as above and fold in chopped cookies for a Ben & Jerry's "chunks" effect.
- Sprinkle blackberries, blueberries, or raspberries on top of the sherbet.

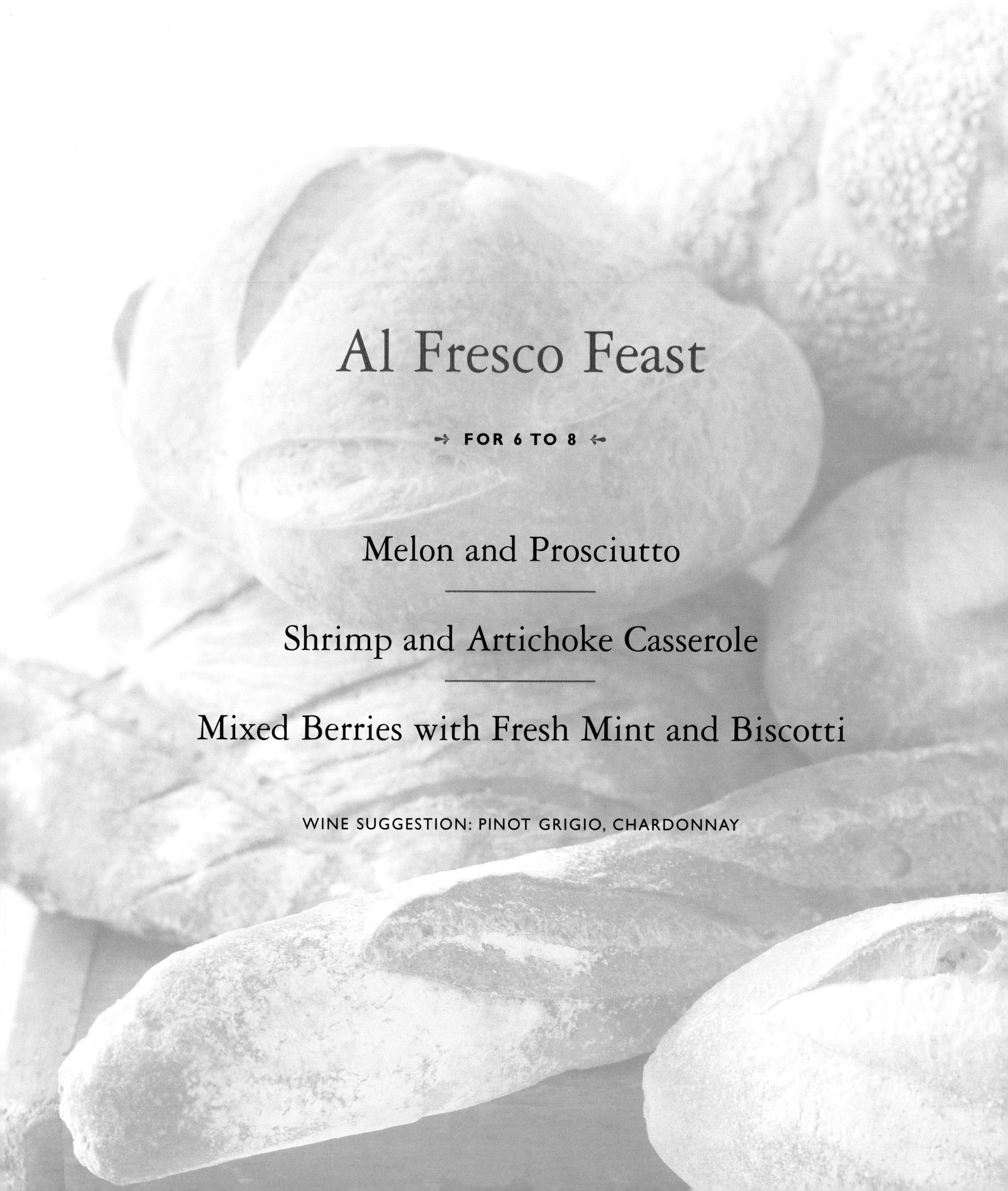

Al Fresco Feast

→ FOR 6 TO 8 ←

Melon and Prosciutto

———————

Shrimp and Artichoke Casserole

———————

Mixed Berries with Fresh Mint and Biscotti

WINE SUGGESTION: PINOT GRIGIO, CHARDONNAY

THIS is an elegantly simple Italian meal, the main dish of which was inspired by the grand matron of northern Italian cuisine, Marcella Hazan. The rest is basically store-bought and a breeze.

HOW TO DO IT:

※ This one is really a question of assembly, so the night before, make sure you have all your ingredients organized and ready to go.

※ Wash and prepare the berries and mint. Slice the melon.

※ An hour before, prepare your platter of melon and prosciutto, assemble the casserole, and prepare your berries in one large pretty glass bowl or in individual bowls, and refrigerate until mealtime.

※ Wrap the bread in foil to warm in the oven, if you like, but it isn't mandatory. *Bellissima!*

melon and prosciutto

SERVES 4
PREP TIME: 5 MINUTES

**1 small melon and 4 ounces prosciutto
Fresh mint for garnish, if desired**

* Choose a ripe, juicy melon, such as cantaloupe or casaba, and slice it into wedges. Cut away the peel or not, as time permits. Most delis and grocery stores these days carry some form of prosciutto, that sublime, salty, thinly sliced Italian ham. But if it isn't available, any thinly sliced salty or smoked ham will do.

* To serve, arrange the melon slices on a platter and drape the prosciutto over them, or wrap the prosciutto around the melon slices, if they're peeled.

* Garnish with fresh mint, chopped or whole, if desired.

shrimp and artichoke casserole

SERVES 4
PREP TIME: 5 MINUTES
COOKING TIME: 10 MINUTES

This one's a last-minute jewel, hear that? I think it's terrific with frozen cooked shrimp, but of course you can use fresh if you like. Our tester mixed the Parmesan in with the shrimp and artichokes by mistake the first time around and said she liked it better that way. Up to you.

* Heat the oven to 450°F.

* Drizzle the baking dish with the olive oil and garlic and place in hot oven for 2 minutes, then remove.

* In a medium bowl, toss the shrimp and artichokes together; add to the baking dish. Sprinkle with mozzarella and bake 5 to 7 minutes if the shrimp are already cooked, or for 15 minutes if the shrimp are raw. The cheese should be bubbly and golden.

* Sprinkle with the Parmesan and a squeeze of lemon, if used, and serve.

NOTE

To thaw frozen shrimp, put them in a colander and run cold water over.

PREP:

11 x 7-inch baking dish

---

2 tablespoons olive oil

1 teaspoon chopped garlic

One 1-pound bag largest-size frozen cooked shrimp, peeled and cleaned

Two 6-ounce jars marinated artichoke hearts

1 cup shredded mozzarella

¼ cup grated Parmesan cheese

½ lemon, if desired

mixed berries with fresh mint and biscotti

3–4 pints fresh berries: strawberries, blueberries, blackberries, raspberries

2 tablespoons sugar

Juice and grated zest of 1 lemon

1 tablespoon chopped fresh mint, plus extra mint sprigs for garnish

1 package biscotti

SERVES 4
PREP TIME: 10 MINUTES

A perfect light summer dessert. The lemon and mint heighten the fresh berry flavor and make it a little different. Prepare it at least an hour, or as much as a day, ahead, so the flavors meld. Perfect with your favorite (store-bought) biscotti or cookies.

* Rinse the berries. Cut the strawberries in half lengthwise.

* Gently combine the berries with the sugar, lemon juice and zest, and chopped mint, and let sit in the refrigerator for at least 1 hour before serving.

* To serve, spoon into bowls or compotes. Garnish with a sprig or two of fresh mint.

VARIATION

These berries would also be good with Killer Coconut Cake (page 165), Cheater's Pound Cake (page 124), or Lemon Sherbet with Gingersnaps (store-bought, page 111).

Fresh Summer Favorites

Fresh Vegetable Basket with Two Dips

―――――――

Crab Cakes

―――――――

Coleslaw

―――――――

Cheater's Pound Cake with Strawberries and Cream

WINE SUGGESTION: VIOGNIER, CHABLIS

I WOULDN'T say we're breaking any new culinary ground here, but sometimes it's refreshing not to, you know? If it ain't broke, don't fix it. When you've got wonderful fresh vegetables, rich savory crabmeat, and the crunchy tang of homemade coleslaw (well, *someone* made it, right?), what more could you want? Strawberry shortcake, you say? Coming right up, only our version is with this sinfully delicious pound cake no one would *ever* know was from a mix. But say you just don't feel like cooking. This entire menu can probably be store-bought, and you just do a little primping and toss a sprig or two of parsley around, and you've got a lovely summer lunch or dinner. These recipes are easily doubled, too.

HOW TO DO IT:

- Up to three days in advance, make the vegetable dips (or buy them), coleslaw (or buy it), and the pound cake (or . . . you get the idea, right?).
- The night before, prepare the veggies and dips, and assemble the crab cakes.
- An hour or so before, prepare the strawberries and whip the cream (or not . . .).

fresh vegetable basket with two dips

PREP:

Large pot for blanching vegetables
Colander

Choose what looks fresh and strikes your fancy: asparagus, bell peppers, broccoli, carrots, cauliflower, celery, cherry tomatoes, endive, fennel, radishes, zucchini. All can be served raw, but if you have time, I think it's better to blanch (or very briefly cook) some of the crunchier, stronger flavored ones like asparagus, broccoli, and cauliflower. It also enhances their color. And of course you don't have to serve these in a basket; any tray or platter will do.

Bring a large pot of water to a boil, and while you're waiting for it, wash and trim the veggies. Add a tablespoon or so of salt to the water just after it begins to boil. Add the asparagus, broccoli, and/or cauliflower and let them cook for 2 to 3 minutes. Drain in the colander and run cold water over to stop the cooking, or plunge the vegetables into ice water.

DIPS FOR FRESH VEGGIES

If you are really pressed, buy one or two good-quality bottled salad dressings, such as Marie's Blue Cheese or Ranch dressing, or any of Annie's Naturals, and brighten them with a good squirt of fresh lemon. Otherwise, here are two you can whip up in a jiffy—and in advance.

curry dip

MAKES I CUP
PREP TIME: 5 MINUTES
MAKE UP TO I WEEK IN ADVANCE.

I cup mayonnaise
2 teaspoons prepared horseradish
I teaspoon lemon juice
I teaspoon curry powder
$1/2$ teaspoon onion powder

* Combine the mayonnaise, horseradish, lemon juice, curry, and onion powder. Cover and refrigerate.

VARIATION

Add I or 2 tablespoons grated onion, I teaspoon grated fresh ginger, and a dash of hot sauce.

avocado dip

MAKES I CUP
PREP TIME: 5 MINUTES
MAKE UP TO I WEEK IN ADVANCE.

Good for veggies and also for chips! If you have a choice, the dark, bumpy-skinned avocados have more flavor than the larger, smooth-skinned ones. We like a smoother consistency for the veggies, a chunkier one for chips.

I cup sour cream
I tablespoon mayonnaise
2 tablespoons fresh lemon juice
I small, ripe avocado, peeled, seeded, and cut into I-inch chunks
I package Italian dressing mix, such as Good Seasons

In a food processor or by hand with a fork or potato masher, combine the sour cream, mayonnaise, lemon juice, avocado, and dressing mix. Cover and refrigerate.

VARIATION

To the avocado dip you might add chopped tomato and/or store-bought real bacon bits on top when serving. You could also add the given amounts of sour cream, mayo, and avocado to $1/2$ cup bottled vinaigrette or our Vinaigrette (page 103) and forgo the packaged Italian dressing mix.

crab cakes

MAKES 8 CRAB CAKES
PREP TIME: 10 MINUTES
CHILLING TIME: 20 MINUTES OR LONGER
COOKING TIME: 12 MINUTES

Fresh crabmeat is definitely a splurge, but it's worth it. And hey, so are you! This excellent recipe comes to us from friend and chef Maurizio Ciminella. We find the mixture easier to handle when well chilled. You can make the patties in the morning or even the night before, but hold off baking them until just before serving. Serve with lemon wedges, tartar sauce (Heinz is good), or Curry Dip (page 121).

* If baking now, heat the oven to 475°F and line the baking pan with foil.

* Combine the crabmeat, onion, mayonnaise, egg, horseradish, and mustard and chill 20 minutes or longer.

* Shape the crab mixture into 8 patties and lightly coat with bread crumbs. Place in the baking pan. If making ahead, cover and refrigerate until baking.

* To bake, drizzle with the melted butter and bake 10 minutes or until lightly browned, 15 minutes if they are straight from the fridge.

PREP:

Medium bowl
Baking pan lined with foil

---

1 pound best lump crabmeat, drained and picked over for bits of shell

1/4 cup minced green onions, white and green parts

1/3 cup mayonnaise

1 egg, lightly beaten

1 teaspoon horseradish

1 teaspoon dry mustard

2 tablespoons bread crumbs or buttery cracker crumbs, such as Ritz

2 tablespoons butter, melted

coleslaw

SERVES 6
PREP TIME: 8 TO 10 MINUTES

A snap to make, and so much better than most sugar-laden commercial varieties.

* In a medium bowl, combine all ingredients. Cover and refrigerate until serving.

One 16-ounce bag coleslaw mix
4 cups shredded fresh cabbage

1/3 cup mayonnaise

2 tablespoons white vinegar

1 tablespoon olive oil

1 teaspoon Dijon mustard

1 teaspoon sugar

1/2 teaspoon whole celery seed

1 teaspoon salt

cheater's pound cake with strawberries and cream

PREP:

Bundt pan, 9 x 13-inch baking dish,
or two 4 x 9-inch loaf pans
Electric mixer, if available

**One 18.5-ounce yellow cake mix,
such as Duncan Hines**

4 large eggs, beaten

I cup sour cream

1/3 cup oil (canola or safflower)

1/4 cup sugar

1/4 cup water

I teaspoon vanilla

I teaspoon almond extract

Easy and the best, from Frances' mother, Ruth Clark. Serve with fresh strawberries and whipped cream (how-to follows). You could also whisk the batter by hand to save mixer cleanup.

* Preheat oven to 375°F. Butter and flour the bottom and all sides of the pan(s).

* Combine the cake mix, eggs, sour cream, oil, sugar, and water, and beat with an electric mixer for 2 minutes (or 3 minutes by hand). Stir in the vanilla and almond extracts.

* Pour into the prepared pan(s) and bake (45 to 50 minutes for Bundt or large baking dish, 35 to 40 minutes for loaf pans), or until a toothpick inserted in the center comes out clean. Cool in pan(s) for 30 minutes before inverting onto a serving plate.

whipped cream—fake it or make it

PREP:

Medium bowl; Electric mixer

FAKE IT

Not as good, I confess, but will do just fine. A bit of orange juice or orange liqueur spiffs it up a bit.

One 8-ounce container nondairy topping,
such as Cool Whip

I tablespoon orange juice or orange liqueur,
such as Grand Marnier or Cointreau

* Whip the juice or liqueur into the topping—and that's that.

MAKE IT

The trick here is to have the cream, the bowl, and the beaters very cold before starting. I stick them in the freezer—but be careful not to let the cream freeze! Whip the cream up to about an hour before serving and refrigerate, or wait until the last minute if you can—it takes 3 to 5 minutes.

I pint whipping cream

2 tablespoons sugar

I teaspoon vanilla

  Pour the cream into a chilled medium bowl and beat at high speed until it begins to thicken. While continuing to beat, add the sugar, then the vanilla.

Jambalaya Buffet

→ FOR 6 TO 8 ←

Savory Cheese Spread

———

Jambalaya

———

Broiled Tomatoes

———

Banana–Brown Sugar "Parfait"

WINE/BEVERAGE SUGGESTION: BEER IS A GOOD CHOICE HERE, OR A RIESLING WINE

FOR SOME reason, when we were testing these menus, this one was a huge hit from start to finish. "You've got to tell us how you made the Jambalaya," they begged. "Old family recipe," we whispered, as we spirited the Rice-a-Roni boxes away.

HOW TO DO IT:

❋ You can make the cheese spread and the dessert a day or two ahead. You can even make the jambalaya a day ahead.

❋ An hour or so before your party, prepare the tomatoes and make the jambalaya, if you haven't already. Both can sit for an hour or so afterward, and all you need to do is reheat.

savory cheese spread

MAKES ABOUT 4 CUPS
PREP TIME: 5 MINUTES
COOKING TIME: 15 MINUTES

Make a day or two ahead and heat before serving. G-o-o-o-d.

❋ Heat oven to 400°F.

❋ Combine all ingredients except lemon juice and salt, and put in a baking dish.

❋ Bake 10 to 15 minutes, until bubbly. Stir in lemon juice and salt. Serve with crackers.

HEAR ALSO WHAT ST. LAURIE SAITH:

St. Laurie would be Laurie Woolever, our ace recipe tester, who offered so many terrific suggestions that we incorporated nearly every one. On this one, however, she waxed particularly eloquent: "Any kind of relatively soft nut, like walnuts or pecans, would be at home in this dip, and maybe a half can of jalapeños for our spicy friends? This seems like a great jumping-off point for lots of great variations—chopped scallions, a spoonful of jarred chopped garlic, 2 tablespoons of salsa, etc." Wow! Thanks, Laurie.

PREP:

Large mixing bowl
Medium baking dish, such as a 1-quart casserole

---

3 cups grated sharp Cheddar cheese

1/2 cup mayonnaise

1 tablespoon grated onion

One 8-ounce can water chestnuts, drained and chopped

1/4 cup drained, chopped sun-dried tomatoes (in oil)

1 tablespoon Worcestershire sauce

1/4 teaspoon cayenne pepper, or to taste

Squirt of fresh lemon juice

Pinch of salt

jambalaya

Large soup pot or Dutch oven

2 tablespoons butter

¼ cup chopped bell pepper,
red or green

¼ cup chopped celery

¼ cup chopped onion

1 box chicken-flavored Rice-a-Roni

2 cups shredded cooked chicken
(optional)

1 pound cubed cooked ham,
about 2 cups

One 1-pound bag cleaned frozen shrimp
(optional)

Ground black pepper

Tabasco or other hot sauce

SERVES 8 TO 10
PREP TIME: 10 MINUTES
COOKING TIME: 20 MINUTES

This is the perfect dish for an informal get-together, and it's always a hit. Get your bell pepper, onion, and celery from the grocery store salad bar—saves you chopping and leftovers. As for the added meats, you can do the ham, chicken, or shrimp alone, or in any combination. I've also tried it with spicy sausage in place of the ham, and it was terrific.

❋ Over high heat, melt the butter in the pot and quickly sauté the bell pepper, celery, and onion, no more than 2 minutes.

❋ Add the Rice-a-Roni rice (but not the seasoning packet) and sauté 30 seconds.

❋ Add 2½ cups water, the Rice-a-Roni seasoning packet, and the chicken (if using). Bring to a boil.

❋ Lower the heat, cover, and simmer 15 minutes.

❋ Add the ham and shrimp (if using) and cook 3 minutes longer if the shrimp were still frozen, but only about 1 minute if they were thawed.

❋ Season with black pepper and hot sauce to taste (we like lots of both), then offer more hot sauce to your guests at serving time.

P·S·S·S·T

Oh, and lose the Rice-a-Roni boxes, wouldja? Just let this be our little secret, okay?

broiled tomatoes

PREP TIME: 10 MINUTES
COOKING TIME: 10 MINUTES

PREP:

Baking pan lined with aluminum foil
or Reynolds Wrap Release non-stick foil
Serrated knife for cutting the tomatoes

4–5 large (or 8–10 small) firm, ripe tomatoes

Salt and freshly ground pepper

1–2 tablespoons white or brown sugar

1/2 cup bread crumbs

1/2 cup grated Parmesan cheese

1/2 teaspoon paprika

4 tablespoons (1/2 stick) butter, melted

A no-brainer accompaniment to casseroles as well as grilled meats, chicken, and seafood. The British even serve them for breakfast. If the tomatoes are small, allow a whole one per person; if large, a half will probably do.

* Line a baking pan or sheet with aluminum foil and grease it with butter, oil, or nonstick spray (unless you're using Release). Preheat the oven to broil.

* Cut the tomatoes in half horizontally and place them cut side up on the baking sheet.

* Sprinkle with salt, pepper, and a pinch of sugar.

* Combine the bread crumbs, cheese, and paprika. Sprinkle this mixture on top of the tomatoes. Drizzle with the melted butter and broil 10 to 12 minutes.

banana–brown sugar "parfait"

SERVES 8 TO 10
PREP TIME: 10 MINUTES
CHILLING TIME: 2 HOURS

This is a variation on a recipe by Delia Smith, England's queen of cooking. We couldn't resist. Takes 10 minutes (or less) and tastes like heaven. If you can get Greek yogurt where you live, it is really good. Vanilla yogurt works as well, and our tester liked the addition of chopped crystallized ginger (¼ cup for the whole batch). Make at least 2 hours ahead.

* Heat the oven to 400°F. Spread the nuts in a baking pan and toast 5 to 7 minutes, checking and shaking pan while they toast.

* Put the yogurt, bananas, and cinnamon in a blender or food processor and pulse to blend—it's okay if there are still a few chunks of banana.

* Spoon the yogurt mixture into bowls or glasses. Top with the brown sugar. Refrigerate for at least 2 hours.

* To serve, sprinkle with the toasted nuts.

PREP:

Blender or food processor
Pan for toasting nuts
8–10 small bowls or wide-mouth glasses

---

1 cup coarsely chopped almonds, pecans, Brazil nuts, or walnuts

4 cups plain yogurt

4 ripe bananas, cut into 1-inch chunks

½ teaspoon cinnamon

1½ cups dark brown sugar

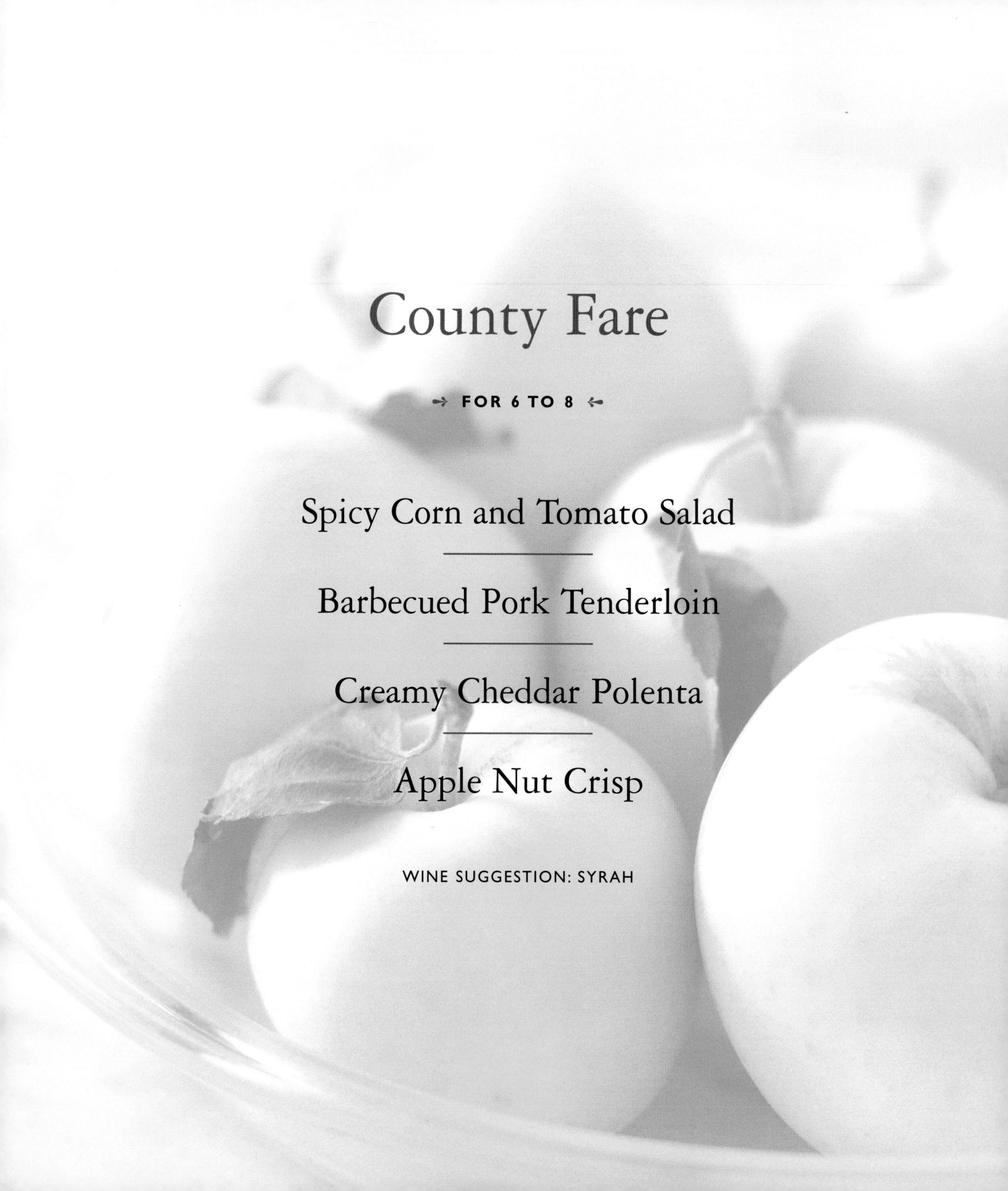

County Fare

FOR 6 TO 8

Spicy Corn and Tomato Salad

Barbecued Pork Tenderloin

Creamy Cheddar Polenta

Apple Nut Crisp

WINE SUGGESTION: SYRAH

THIS menu is a little different, but believe me, it's a sure thing! Pork tenderloin is one of our favorites—lean, flavorful, versatile. I don't know why you don't see it just everywhere. Hmm. All the more reason why your guests will think you're so original and creative. And the house will smell heavenly while you're cooking it.

HOW TO DO IT:

❋ In the days before your party, do your setups: plates, glasses, flatware, linens, table, bar, buffet, decorations. Doing a little at a time keeps it manageable and stress free. And if something needs pressing or wiping or shining, you have time to do it.

❋ The night before or morning of, make the Spicy Corn and Tomato Salad, marinate the pork, make the polenta, and prepare the dessert—but keep the topping separate. Cover and refrigerate everything.

❋ Two hours ahead of party time, take out the pork and dessert.

❋ An hour ahead, begin grilling the pork and bake the dessert (having added the topping, of course!). Take out the polenta if you've made it ahead, or make it now if you haven't.

❋ Fifteen to thirty minutes ahead, take out the corn and tomato salad and prepare as directed.

❋ If you are doing all this on the fly, that's okay, too. You can grill the pork, make the polenta, bake the dessert, and plate the (prepared) salad within an hour of your guests arriving, while they're all standing around in the kitchen. This menu is goof-proof enough that a distraction or twelve won't be a problem. My kinda cookin'!

spicy corn and tomato salad

Three 7-ounce cans large-kernel
or shoepeg corn

I green, yellow, or red bell pepper,
chopped

I medium red onion, finely chopped

I tablespoon finely chopped (canned)
jalapeño peppers, or I finely chopped
fresh jalapeño

¼ cup sour cream, or more for a
creamier consistency

¼ cup mayonnaise

I teaspoon whole celery seed

½ teaspoon dry mustard, or
I teaspoon prepared Dijon mustard

½ teaspoon chili powder

Salt and black pepper, to taste

6–8 Roma tomatoes

Bibb or other leaf lettuce for serving

Cilantro to garnish, if desired

MAKES ABOUT TWELVE ½-CUP SERVINGS
PREP TIME: 30 MINUTES

This is dee-lish and great made ahead because the flavors have a chance to meld. It looks like a lot of ingredients, but there's nothing exotic. If you're down to the wire and missing something like celery seed or dry mustard, don't sweat it. It'll still be good.

✳ In a large bowl combine the corn, bell pepper, onion, jalapeño, sour cream, mayonnaise, celery seed, mustard, and chili powder. Cover and refrigerate until serving, letting it come to room temp or close to it beforehand—this enhances the flavors.

✳ Season generously with salt and pepper, but only just before serving. Otherwise the salt will draw out the moisture from the vegetables and make the salad runny.

✳ To serve, slice the Roma tomatoes into rounds and spread on a plate—on lettuce leaves, if you like. Spoon corn salad over and sprinkle with chopped cilantro, if using.

barbecued pork tenderloin

PREP TIME: 10 MINUTES
GRILLING TIME: 40 MINUTES

This is a specialty of our friend Rex Fuqua. The dish is a family favorite—and so is Rex, come to think of it. You can easily increase or decrease this and still use the same amount of marinade. Figure on about 6 ounces of meat per person. Which barbecue sauce to choose from the oodles out there? Read the labels and select the one that most appeals to you. For a sweeter sauce, choose one with brown sugar and/or molasses; for a spicier sauce, go with a more vinegary base, or one that says "hot and spicy."

* Combine the barbecue sauce and salad dressing in a bowl or plastic bag and add the tenderloins. Refrigerate and marinate for 2 hours to overnight. Let come to room temperature before cooking.

* Preheat the oven to 400°F, or prepare the grill.

* Remove the tenderloins from the marinade and pat dry. Rub all over with salt and pepper. (Reserve extra marinade if you like; see "Feeling Saucy?")

* Roast or grill the tenderloins for about 40 minutes. They are done when a meat thermometer reads 135°F and the meat is pale pink in the center. Let rest 10 minutes before cutting—this allows the juices to be absorbed into the meat while it finishes cooking.

* To make a sauce from the leftover marinade, pour it into a small pan over medium-high heat and boil it for about 3 minutes. This will get rid of any lingering bacteria from the raw meat. Pour the sauce over the meat or put it in a separate bowl to pass.

PREP:

Roasting pan, stovetop grill pan, or grill

---

1 bottle (16 ounces) prepared barbecue sauce

1 bottle (16 ounces) prepared Italian salad dressing

3–4 pork tenderloins (3–4 pounds total)

Salt and black pepper, to taste

FEELING SAUCY?

If you want to jazz up the marinade, add a handful of chopped herbs such as rosemary, basil, cilantro, or mint, or a tablespoon or two of chopped garlic. If you want to heat it up, you could add a tablespoon of red pepper flakes or a few crushed, dried chiles.

creamy cheddar polenta

2½ cups water

2½ cups milk

I cup polenta or coarse yellow cornmeal

1½ cups grated sharp Cheddar cheese

3 teaspoons salt

Paprika, if desired

MAKES ABOUT EIGHT ⅓-CUP SERVINGS
PREP TIME: 20 MINUTES

If you can't make this at the last minute, it's perfectly fine to make ahead and reheat. Feel free to be creative with the cheese. A little grated Parmesan or Romano in the mix would give it a little more kick.

* In a large saucepan, bring the water and milk just to the boil. Slowly add the polenta or cornmeal, stirring constantly. Lower the heat and continue to cook and stir until thickened, about 10 minutes.

* Stir in the cheese and salt.

* To serve, sprinkle with paprika for color, if desired.

TIP

Most grocery stores stock polenta that comes in a box. If you like, use that and follow the package directions (easy), stirring in your cheese and seasonings at the end.

apple nut crisp

SERVES 8 TO 10
PREP: FOOD PROCESSOR OR PASTRY BLENDER
PREP TIME: 20 MINUTES
BAKING TIME: 45 TO 50 MINUTES

With a crunchy, nutty topping that beats a boring old crust any day.

* Heat the oven to 375°F.

* In an ungreased baking dish or casserole, stir the lemon juice into the partially thawed apples.

* In a medium bowl or food processor, combine the sugar, flour, cinnamon, nutmeg, and salt.

* Using a pastry blender or the processor on "pulse," cut in the butter until the mixture forms coarse, lumpy crumbs. Stir in the oats and nuts.

* Sprinkle the mixture evenly over the apples. Bake 45 to 50 minutes. Serve warm or at room temperature—and with a big scoop of vanilla ice cream, if you like. Yummy.

PREP:

7 x 11-inch baking dish or 2-quart casserole

1 tablespoon lemon juice

Two 10-ounce packages frozen scalloped apples, such as Stouffer's or Boston Market, partially thawed

1/2 cup packed brown sugar (light or dark)

1/3 cup flour

1 teaspoon cinnamon

1/2 teaspoon ground nutmeg

1/2 teaspoon salt

6 tablespoons (3/4 stick) butter, chopped in small pieces, very cold

1/3 cup regular (old-fashioned) oats, raw, such as Quaker oats

1/3 cup chopped almonds or pecans, toasted

French Country Comfort

→ FOR 6 TO 8 ←

Veal Stew

———

Salad with Fresh Herbs and Vinaigrette

———

Cheese Plate

———

Pumpkin Crème Brûlée

WINE SUGGESTION: MERLOT, BEAUJOLAIS

I KNOW we are all about cooking off the cuff here, and this stew is just a little more involved, but if you'll bear with me, you won't be sorry. Just because this takes a little more time doesn't mean it's hard to do. And apart from broiling the brown sugar on top of the crème brûlée, the stew involves the only cooking there is! Now that wasn't so bad, was it? Oh, and did I mention your guests will think they've died and gone to the Cordon Bleu?

WELL BREAD

I prefer to serve the bread with the cheese and salad, but if you also want bread with the stew—to soak up the juices—I won't argue with you.

JUST A THOUGHT

It's always nice to set the bowl or soup plate on a charger or dinner plate so you have a place to rest your spoon between bites. I then sometimes clear the bowls and serve the salad and cheese on the plate that's left. Streamlines things a little, ya know?

TIP

While you're warming the bread, you might want to warm the stew bowls in the oven along with it. That's a nice touch.

HOW TO DO IT:

* Make the stew and the crème part of the dessert up to three days in advance.

* Prepare your table and bar, including plates, glasses, flatware, and napkins.

* About an hour before your guests arrive, take the stew out of the fridge and begin to warm it over very low heat, giving it a stir every now and then.

* Sprinkle the brown sugar over the crème and "brûlée" it, leaving it at room temp when finished.

* Twenty to thirty minutes before you're ready to eat, put your cheeses on a board or plate, and cover with a barely damp kitchen towel to keep the cheese from drying out. Dress the salad. Wrap the bread in foil and toss it in the oven on low heat.

veal stew

SERVES 6 TO 8
PREP TIME: 15 MINUTES
COOKING TIME: 1 TO 2 HOURS

PREP:

Dutch oven or large soup pot
Large sauté or frying pan
Microplane grater or lemon zester

¼ cup olive oil

2 pounds veal, cut into 1-inch cubes

Salt and ground black pepper

One 9-ounce package frozen small
or pearl onions, thawed, or
2 cups coarsely chopped yellow onions

1 tablespoon chopped garlic

1 cup white wine

3 cups chicken stock

1–2 sprigs fresh rosemary,
or 1 teaspoon dried

Grated zest of 1 small or ½ large lemon

1 pound fresh mushrooms

One 15-ounce can white beans, such as
Great Northern or white kidney,
rinsed and drained

½ cup grated Swiss or Gruyère cheese

Everyone always wants seconds and the recipe. Granted it's a little more involved than most of the recipes in this book, but it's really easy. You can make the stew up to three days ahead, or freeze it up to three months. If you want to simplify further, skip the lemon, mushrooms, and cheese, which means you'll skip two of the cooking steps. The flavor will be less complex, but it will still be yummy. Promise.

* Heat the oil in a Dutch oven or a heavy soup pot over medium-high heat. Meanwhile, liberally season the veal by rubbing it all over with salt and freshly ground pepper.

* You may need to do this in batches: Add the veal to the pot and sear it on all sides, 5 to 7 minutes. Remove from the pot and set aside.

* In the same pot you used for the veal, still on medium-high heat, sauté the onions 5 to 10 minutes or until they begin to brown. If necessary, add a little water or stock.

* Lower the heat to medium and add the garlic, sautéing for 1 to 2 minutes; then add the wine and cook for about 2 minutes.

* Add the stock, veal, rosemary, and lemon zest. Lower the heat, cover, and simmer for at least 1 hour and up to 2 hours, checking and stirring occasionally.

* In the other pan, sauté the mushrooms on medium-high for 2 to 3 minutes. Set aside until the stew is ready.

* Add the beans and the mushrooms with their cooking juices into the stew. At this point, the stew may be refrigerated or frozen.

* When ready to serve, stir in the grated cheese until it melts into the stew. Serve immediately.

salad with fresh herbs and vinaigrette

Selection of fresh herbs, such as parsley, dill, chives, marjoram, basil, thyme, oregano, or tarragon

Two 5-ounce bags prewashed salad greens

Vinaigrette Dressing (page 103)

If you can find the organic greens already mixed with fresh herbs, use those. If not, add your own. If fresh herbs are hard to come by where you live, don't worry; a salad is a salad, and it'll be just as good without them. The addition of store-bought croutons, toasted nuts, or pumpkin seeds is good, too.

✳ Wash and dry the herbs. Chop the parsley, dill, and chives. Pull the leaves from the marjoram, basil, thyme, oregano, and tarragon. Add to the lettuces in a large salad bowl.

✳ Anywhere from 2 to 20 minutes before serving, toss the salad with vinaigrette. Some chefs even season their greens with salt and pepper before putting on the dressing—gives them a little ooh-la-la.

cheese plate

Entire books have been written about cheese, but I haven't had time to read one. I do think a cheese course at the end of a meal is a sophisticated, Euro-type thing to do. Serve with crackers or, as the French do, with French bread. Another thing the French do is serve the salad and cheese together, after the main course. Crazy, huh? But try it sometime; it works especially well with a meal like this one, and it gives you a little break between a hearty main course and a rich dessert.

For simplicity's sake, I like to have three or four cheeses, each of a different type, but it's your party—have what you want. In other words, the following is merely a suggestion, in quantities of ¼ to ½ pound each:

Soft tangy cheese, such as goat cheese

Soft creamy cheese, such as Brie or Camembert

Hard cheese, such as Swiss, Emmentaler, or Gruyère

Blue cheese, such as Roquefort or Stilton

pumpkin crème brûlée

SERVES 10 TO 12
PREP TIME: 10 MINUTES
REFRIGERATION TIME: 2 HOURS
BAKING TIME: 3 TO 4 MINUTES

If you're out of vanilla or other spices, not to worry—make it without. You can make the crème the night before and bake just before serving, which takes about 3 minutes.

* Combine the cream or milk, pumpkin, pudding mix, vanilla, cinnamon, and nutmeg, and spoon the mixture into cups or ramekins. Place the filled cups in a 9 × 13-inch baking pan. Refrigerate about 2 hours, or until set.

* Adjust the oven rack to the top position and preheat the broiler.

* Sprinkle the brown sugar evenly over the pudding. Put two handfuls of ice cubes in the pan between the ramekins and fill the pan halfway with cold water. Broil 3 to 4 minutes, or until the sugar is browned and bubbly. Leave at room temperature until serving time.

PREP:

Large bowl
Electric mixer or whisk
10 to 12 coffee cups or small ramekins
9 x 13-inch baking pan

2 cups heavy cream or half-and-half, or one 12-ounce can evaporated milk, chilled

One 12-ounce can cooked plain pumpkin, chilled

Two 4-serving-size packages instant vanilla pudding mix

1 teaspoon vanilla

1 teaspoon cinnamon

¼ teaspoon nutmeg

⅓ cup brown sugar

Pizza Pizzazz

Pizza, Pizza, Pizza

———————

Green Salad with Oranges, Red Onion, and Mint

———————

Pasta Salad

———————

Fruit and Chocolate "Fun-do"

WINE SUGGESTION: CHIANTI

I DID this simple, chic, and fun party at my home and loved everything about it. Later we re-created it on the show and got so many requests for it that we had to include it here. The secret weapon? Five little words: *Pepperidge Farm puff pastry dough.* Yeah! What I love about it, apart from the fact that it's already made, is that it is light and flaky, so the toppings are the focal point. The pizza slices literally melt in your mouth, so your guests get full on your yummy herbs and toppings and not on the "bread." You can serve this any way you want, and everything can be made well in advance. I usually start by popping four ready-to-bake pizzas in the oven as the guests arrive. By the time they have their first cocktail and catch up on the latest gossip, the first round of pizzas is ready to serve. And by virtue of their delicate crusts, they easily double as hors d'oeuvre. But more importantly, your guests get the idea of the party right off the bat—and the fun begins. As the party progresses, you can assemble the pizzas as you go or lay out the toppings and let people make them themselves, which becomes delightfully interactive.

HOW TO DO IT:

* As much as two days in advance, prepare the pizza crusts, cover, and refrigerate.

* Assemble the topping ingredients you want and put them in bowls so they are easily accessible and ready to go.

* Prepare the deli-bought pasta salad on a platter, cover, and refrigerate.

* Prepare the ingredients and the dressing for the green salad. If you like, select them from the salad bar and put them in a container separate from the lettuce leaves. Then you're ready to toss and go.

* Wash, peel, and dry the fruit for the chocolate "fun-do."

* Set up the bar and set up the plates, napkins, and utensils buffet-style.

* An hour before your guests arrive, set up your pizza bar and begin assembling your first batch of pizzas. Twenty minutes before, take out the pasta salad and the fixings for the green salad.

* When your guests arrive, pop the first batch of pizzas in the oven. Take my advice and use a timer. You know how you might get to talking and pretty soon someone says "Is something burning?" Um-hmm. Let one of your guests toss the salad just before the pizzas are done.

pizza, pizza, pizza

Platter or cookie sheet for storing crusts

Wax or parchment paper

Cookie sheet(s) or round baking pan(s)

9-inch pie crust shield (see Note, opposite)

Bowls and serving utensils for sauces and toppings

MAKES EIGHT 9-INCH ROUND OR EIGHT 14 X 10-INCH
RECTANGULAR PIZZAS

PREP TIME: 20 TO 40 MINUTES

BAKING TIME: 15 MINUTES

I have found that each person will consume at least the equivalent of one small pizza, but realistically, they're so darn great, people can usually eat two—especially the guys. The "recipes" here are just suggestions. Feel free to mix and match!

PIZZA CRUSTS

8 puff pastry sheets (4 packages of the Pepperidge Farm kind, which has 2 sheets per package)

* Thaw the pastry according to package instructions. Unfold the crusts and either leave them in the rectangular shape or cut them into rounds using the pie crust shield or a round plate as a template and cutting around it with a knife.

* Stack the crusts on a platter or cookie sheet with a layer of wax or parchment paper between each crust. Refrigerate until ready to use, up to 2 days in advance.

ASSEMBLE, BAKE, AND SERVE!

* Preheat oven to 400°F.

* Assemble ingredients on unbaked crust.

* Lift the crust to the baking pan with the wax or parchment paper, leaving the paper on the bottom. Bake 15 minutes.

* When done, slide the pizza off the wax or parchment paper onto a platter, pizza stone, or tin pedestals, which can be found in most restaurant supply stores.

PIZZA COMBOS

Use your creativity and let your guests use theirs! You can follow our suggested combos or create your own. The good news is cooking sauce is not required. In the refrigerated section of your supermarket, there are pizza and pasta sauces just waiting for you. Contadina is one brand I like, but there are several. For variety, choose a red tomato-based sauce, a green pesto sauce, and a white Alfredo sauce—the colors of the Italian flag! Since you'll be using only about ¼ cup per pizza, a little goes a long way. To set up your pizza bar, place sauces and toppings in individual bowls on your kitchen counter.

NOTE

To cut the crust into rounds, you need something to use as a big cookie cutter. The best thing I've found is a 9-inch pie crust shield, available at any cooking store for about three bucks and change.

PAN-ORAMA

For pizzas, I prefer the round baking (pizza!) pans to the rectangular ones—more authentic, ya know? They're inexpensive and usually available in the grocery store. Or you can find real pizza pans in kitchen shops.

POINTS FOR PRESENTATION

I line my serving dishes with lace paper doilies for that sort of fresh-baked pastry look. Love that. If you don't have pedestal plates, try three or four overturned drinking glasses with your doily-lined glass plate on top, and there you have it.

GUARD THE BORDERS

When spooning sauce onto the raw pastry dough, leave at least 1 inch all the way around the edges uncoated. This will puff up beautifully, forming a delicious-looking crust. Topping quantities listed are for a single pizza, so increase your amounts accordingly—and they don't have to be exact.

smoked chicken with rosemary

Find smoked chicken (or turkey) in the deli section of your supermarket. Shred by hand for a gourmet look.

1/4 cup prepared Alfredo sauce

1/3 cup shredded smoked chicken

1 tablespoon fresh chopped rosemary,
  or 1/2 teaspoon dried

1 tablespoon pine nuts, toasted in the oven
  or sautéed in olive oil

1/4 cup caramelized onions (how-to follows)

1/4 cup crumbled feta or goat cheese

* To make caramelized onions, slice one large red onion into thin rings and sauté over medium heat in 1 tablespoon olive oil, 1 tablespoon molasses (optional), and 1 teaspoon balsamic vinegar, until the onions are a deep golden brown. Takes about 15 minutes. You can do this ahead by a day or two and keep them covered in a bowl in the fridge.

* Spread pizza crust with Alfredo sauce, leaving a 1-inch border all the way around.

* Sprinkle with remaining ingredients, ending with cheese.

* Bake according to directions on page 148.

pesto, arugula, mushroom, and prosciutto

Sauté the mushrooms beforehand in a little olive oil and season with salt and pepper.

1/4 cup prepared pesto sauce

Thinly sliced provolone cheese
  to cover crust

1 small bunch arugula

1/4 cup sliced mushrooms

3 or 4 slices prosciutto or other
  thinly sliced salty ham

5 or 6 shavings Parmesan cheese

* Top the pizza with sauce and provolone cheese, remembering to leave a 1-inch border of crust uncovered so it will puff. Bake according to directions on page 148.

* Remove the pizza from the oven and top with fresh arugula, mushrooms, prosciutto, and Parmesan.

sun-dried tomato, meatloaf, and olive

Buy prepared meatloaf, or substitute a mild, cooked sausage. Buy sun-dried tomatoes packed in oil, or soften the dried ones by pouring boiling water over them and letting them sit for 10 minutes or so. And by all means use roasted red peppers from a jar and frozen asparagus, which needs thawing but not cooking. Pizza cheese comes packaged and shredded—the Sargento brand is good.

1/4 cup prepared tomato sauce

4 ounces meatloaf pieces, chopped

1 tablespoon chopped sun-dried tomatoes

1 tablespoon chopped black Kalamata olives

1 tablespoon sliced or chopped roasted red peppers

1/4 cup chopped cooked asparagus tips

1/4 cup shredded pizza cheese

* Spread the crust with tomato sauce, leaving a 1-inch border all the way around.

* Sprinkle with remaining ingredients, ending with cheese.

TRY SOME MORE OF THESE COMBINATIONS:

- Instead of a sauce, drizzle the crust with olive oil and top with any or all of the following:

  Goat cheese
  Fresh sage
  Caramelized onions
  Toasted walnuts
  Roasted peppers (from a jar)
  Herbes de Provence

- Or try a tangy Thai seafood pizza with:

  Pesto sauce
  Baby shrimp (from a can, rinsed and drained)
  Tuna chunks (from a can, rinsed and drained)
  Water chestnuts (sliced, rinsed, and drained)
  1 teaspoon grated lemon zest
  Halved roasted garlic cloves (the Christopher Ranch brand in a jar in the produce section)
  Asparagus tips
  Diced red onion
  Grated Gruyère cheese
  Chopped mint (fresh or dried)
  Old Bay seasoning
  Thai peanut sauce, drizzled on top
  Chopped fresh green onions, for garnish

green salad with oranges, red onion, and mint

²/₃ cup olive oil

2 tablespoons balsamic vinegar or fresh lemon juice, or a combination

2 bags prewashed salad greens, or equivalent

1 or 2 cans Mandarin orange slices, rinsed and drained

1 cup frozen peas, thawed under hot water

1 medium red onion, thinly sliced

1 tablespoon minced fresh mint

1 hard-boiled egg, chopped

¼ cup crumbled bacon (bits from a jar, or 4 slices cooked)

SERVES 8
PREP TIME: 10 MINUTES

* Whisk the olive oil and vinegar and/or lemon juice, or shake up in a jar and set aside.

* Combine the remaining salad ingredients and toss with the dressing.

pasta salad

Pasta salad (store-bought)

Romaine lettuce

Parmesan cheese

Italian parsley

* Almost every grocery store has a cold pasta salad you can serve as is or doctor up to your own taste. Line a large platter with romaine leaves and mound the pasta salad on top. Sprinkle with grated Parmesan cheese and chopped Italian parsley. Allow ⅓ to ½ cup serving per person.

fruit and chocolate "fun-do"

If you have a fondue pot, use it. If you don't, use a double boiler and, while you're serving, turn the stove heat on and off as necessary. You could also use the microwave to keep the chocolate soft.

FOR THE CHOCOLATE:

✳ Slowly melt together the butter and chocolate. Keep warm while dipping.

FOR THE FRUIT:

Follow our suggestions or try your own. Pineapple and fresh figs are interesting, and certain dried fruits—apricots, mangos, and pears, for example—are excellent.

✳ In a tall container or glass, place long wooden skewers to make dipping easy for your guests.

✳ Arrange the fruit on a platter (a black lacquer tray would be pretty) and place near the "fun-do." Dip away!

VARIATION

If you don't want to do the dipping bit, line a cookie sheet with parchment or wax paper or Release nonstick aluminum foil. Lay out the fruit in a single layer, drizzle with the melted chocolate, and allow it to harden 15 minutes or so. Refrigerating would speed the process. To serve, arrange the fruit pieces on a doily-lined platter or glass serving plate.

FOR THE CHOCOLATE:

1 pound semisweet chocolate

4 tablespoons butter

FOR THE FRUIT:

4 oranges, sectioned and peeled

1 pint fresh strawberries, washed and dried, stems intact

Steakhouse Special

→ **FOR 6 TO 8** ←

Spinach, Bacon, and Mushroom Salad

Marinated Steak

(Not Your Mama's) Macaroni and Cheese

Chocolate Fudge Pie

WINE SUGGESTION: CABERNET SAUVIGNON, ZINFANDEL

THIS one's a Christopher Special—a big, hearty meal that includes everyone's favorites. What's not to love here? Cook the steak in a grill pan or skillet, or let Sweetie do the outdoor grill thing on his own. The rest of the meal you assemble and then sit back and soak up the compliments—between the requests for seconds, that is.

* The pie can be made up to three days in advance.

* The day before or morning of, assemble the salad ingredients, marinate the steak, and assemble the mac and cheese. (Hide those Stouffer's boxes!)

spinach, bacon, and mushroom salad

SERVES 6
PREP TIME: 10 MINUTES

Pre- to be free: Prewashed spinach, precooked bacon, presliced mushrooms (fresh from the salad bar or canned). And you've already got some of that great Vinaigrette Dressing in the fridge, right?

* In a large salad bowl, combine the spinach, bacon, and mushrooms. Pour the dressing over and toss.

VARIATION

Sometimes spinach salads are served with a warm dressing, which wilts it slightly. Why not give it a try? Just warm your dressing for 30 to 60 seconds in the microwave before pouring it over and tossing your salad.

One 16-ounce bag prewashed spinach

6 pieces bacon, cooked and crumbled

1 1/2 cups sliced mushrooms, fresh or canned (drain and rinse the canned ones)

Vinaigrette Dressing (page 103)

NOTE

If you use canned mushrooms, drain and rinse them first. If you are making a warm dressing and using precooked bacon, warm it up in a frying pan or for 15 seconds on a paper towel in the microwave.

marinated steak

¼ **cup soy sauce**

¼ **cup sherry**

¼ **cup honey**

I tablespoon meat tenderizer

I tablespoon salt

3 pounds top round steak, I ½ inches thick

Salt and ground black pepper

SERVES 6 TO 8
PREP TIME: 5 MINUTES
MARINATING TIME: 6 HOURS
COOKING TIME: 12 MINUTES FOR MEDIUM RARE

This one sizzles! Let the beef marinate for at least 6 hours. Directions below are for pan-searing, but if you're in the mood to fire up the grill, do it! You could also use an indoor grill or stovetop grill pan.

✻ In a shallow pan or sealable plastic bag big enough to hold the beef, combine the soy sauce, sherry, honey, tenderizer, and salt. Add the beef and let marinate 6 hours or longer, turning occasionally.

✻ Put a large, heavy skillet on high heat. It's hot enough when a drop of water on it sizzles like crazy. Turn up the exhaust fan, because it may get a little smoky. (Or simply use your grill.)

✻ Remove the meat from the marinade, pat it dry, and season with salt and pepper. Add the meat to the hot skillet and, for medium rare, cook about 7 minutes on the first side, 5 minutes on the second side. Make a little cut in the center to check. The meat should be a little underdone because it keeps cooking after you take it out. Let it rest for 5 minutes before carving diagonally, across the grain, in ¼-inch slices.

✻ To make a sauce from the leftover marinade, boil it on the stovetop for about 3 minutes.

PSSST

Want to take a shortcut with a bottled marinade?
Step right this way. . . .

LEFTOVERS?

Hey! How about making the Grilled Beef Salad (page 102)?

(not your mama's) macaroni and cheese

SERVES 8
PREP TIME: 10 MINUTES
COOKING TIME: 20 MINUTES

This is one of my favorites in the "Let's don't and say we did" department. Everyone loves it.

✳ Heat the oven to 400°F.

✳ Thaw the macaroni in the microwave, about 3 minutes on high (but time varies with the strength of the oven).

✳ In a 2-quart casserole, gently combine the macaroni, peppers, blue and Parmesan cheeses, and hot sauce. Use a paper towel to wipe the inside of the casserole above the macaroni so it doesn't look yucky after it's baked.

✳ Sprinkle the top with the Cheddar cheese and paprika. Bake, uncovered, about 15 minutes, or until cheese is melted and bubbly.

PREP:

2-quart casserole

Two 12-ounce packages frozen macaroni and cheese, such as Stouffer's

½ cup chopped roasted red peppers

¼ cup crumbled blue cheese

¼ cup grated Parmesan cheese

Dash of Tabasco or other hot sauce

¼ cup grated sharp Cheddar cheese

Paprika

chocolate fudge pie

PREP:

9-inch pie crust (see YO!)

One 9-inch pie crust

Two 1-ounce squares unsweetened chocolate

½ cup (1 stick) butter

¼ cup milk

1 cup sugar

1 egg, beaten

1 tablespoon flour

1 teaspoon vanilla

¼ teaspoon salt

Sheer chocolate heaven.

* Heat the oven to 400°F. Press the pie crust into your pie plate.

* Lightly prick the pie crust and bake 5 minutes. Let cool.

* Lower the oven heat to 375°F.

* In a medium saucepan over low heat, melt the chocolate and butter. Remove from the heat.

* Combine the milk, sugar, egg, flour, vanilla, and salt. Stir into the chocolate mixture.

* Pour the filling into the pie shell and bake 30 minutes.

YO!

For that homemade look, Pillsbury makes a ready-made pie crust dough that you unfold and press into your own pie plate. They come two to a box and are found in the refrigerated foods section.

TIP

To intensify the chocolate flavor, add ½ teaspoon instant coffee granules and/or ¼ teaspoon cinnamon. Love that.

Bollywood Boulevard

→ **FOR 6 TO 8** ←

Fruit Salad with Spiced Yogurt Dressing

—————

Chicken Curry with Rice "Pea-laf"

—————

Steamed Broccoli

—————

Killer Coconut Cake

WINE SUGGESTION: SAUVIGNON BLANC

HAVE some fun with this one! Commune with your inner maharajah. Dress up, decorate, go kitsch. You won't be, ah, sari! Curry freezes well and is great for a crowd. The condiments can be as simple or as elaborate as you like. The fruit salad is a lovely accompaniment, but if you'd rather have a green salad, either would be good with the curry. You could buy a prepared fruit salad and make only the yogurt dressing. Steamed broccoli is available at shops offering prepared foods. Also, if there's no time for cake-baking, get thee to a bakery.

❋ Prepare the curry as far in advance as you like and freeze, or store in the fridge for up to three days.

❋ Bake the cake up to three days in advance.

❋ The day before, make the fruit salad and the broccoli, and prepare the condiments you'll be serving with the curry.

❋ The rice is the only thing to do at the last minute. Even it can be cooked up to an hour before and left to stand at room temperature.

fruit salad with spiced yogurt dressing

PREP:

Small bowl for mixing dressing
Larger bowl to hold salad

---

1 cup plain yogurt

1 tablespoon honey

1–2 tablespoons orange juice or orange liqueur (such as Grand Marnier)

¾ teaspoon cinnamon

¼ teaspoon nutmeg

6 cups assorted chopped fresh fruits such as apples, oranges, bananas, pineapple, pears, peaches, strawberries, mango, papaya

Bibb lettuce for serving

⅓ cup chopped almonds, toasted

⅓ cup coconut, for garnish, if desired

SERVES 6 TO 8
PREP TIME: 20 MINUTES

Vanilla yogurt would work here as well, but you might want to omit the honey. A tablespoon of minced crystallized ginger would be a nice addition, too.

✳ In a small bowl combine the yogurt, honey, juice or liqueur to taste, and spices. Refrigerate.

✳ If you haven't already, chop or slice the fruit into bite-size pieces, saving the bananas until the last minute so they won't get brown and mushy. If you're using apples, toss them with a bit of fresh lemon juice to keep them from turning brown.

✳ To serve, place lettuce leaves on a large platter or individual salad plates and add fruit. Spoon yogurt dressing over, then sprinkle with toasted almonds and coconut.

chicken curry with rice "pea-laf"

I small onion, chopped, about I cup

I tablespoon olive oil or butter

One 10½-ounce can cream of chicken soup

½ cup mayonnaise

1½ cups chicken stock

2 teaspoons curry powder

Two 10-ounce packages oven-roasted chicken, such as Perdue Short Cuts, or 3–4 cups cooked, shredded chicken

1½–2 cups quick-cooking rice

One 10-ounce package frozen peas, thawed

Two 1-ounce packages golden raisins

⅛ teaspoon cayenne pepper, or to taste

SERVES 6 TO 8
PREP TIME: 5 MINUTES
COOKING TIME: 20 MINUTES

If you want to make this a little greener, prepare a package of frozen broccoli and serve it with or in the curry. I've done it both ways. Serve with condiments set alongside in their own small bowls—chutney, chopped peanuts, tomatoes, toasted coconut, and chopped black olives all work.

✳ In a large saucepan over medium-high heat, sauté the onion in the oil or butter until soft, about 5 to 6 minutes.

✳ Whisk in the cream of chicken soup and mayonnaise, then the stock and curry powder. Bring to a boil.

✳ Lower the heat and stir in the chicken. Cover and simmer over low heat 10 to 15 minutes, or however long it takes to do the following:

✳ Make the rice according to package instructions.

✳ Stir the thawed peas into the cooked rice.

✳ Stir raisins and cayenne into curry.

✳ Serve the curry on top of or alongside the rice, with condiments as desired.

killer coconut cake

MAKES ONE 9 X 13-INCH CAKE
PREP TIME: 10 MINUTES FOR THE CAKE, 10 MINUTES FOR THE FROSTING
BAKING TIME: 40 MINUTES

The title says it all. This cake is so moist that weight watchers may skip the frosting and sprinkle a little powdered sugar over the top (every little bit helps, right?). This can also be whisked by hand, if you don't want the mixer mess to clean up.

✳ Grease and flour a 9 × 13-inch baking pan. Preheat the oven to 350°F.

✳ Combine the eggs, oil, sour cream, and coconut milk. Stir in the cake mix and beat 2 minutes.

✳ Add the lemon juice and zest, vanilla, and almond extract, and then stir in the coconut.

✳ Try not to eat half the batter before pouring it into the prepared pan. Bake 40 to 45 minutes, or until a toothpick inserted in the center comes out clean.

✳ Let cool completely before icing with Cream Cheese Frosting.

Cream Cheese Frosting

Two 8-ounce packages cream cheese, at room temperature
1 cup (2 sticks) butter, at room temperature
One 16-ounce box confectioner's sugar
1 tablespoon lemon juice
1 teaspoon vanilla
1/2 teaspoon almond extract
1 cup coconut

✳ With an electric mixer, blend the cream cheese, butter, and sugar.

✳ Add the lemon juice, vanilla, and almond extract.

✳ Frost the cake. Sprinkle the top with the coconut.

PREP:

9 x 13-inch baking pan
Mixing bowl
Electric mixer
Microplane grater for lemon zest

---

3 eggs, lightly beaten

1/4 cup canola or safflower oil

1 cup (8 ounces) sour cream

3/4 cup unsweetened coconut milk

One 18.5-ounce box yellow cake mix

Juice and grated zest of 1 lemon

1 teaspoon vanilla

1 teaspoon almond extract

1 cup coconut

Cream Cheese Frosting

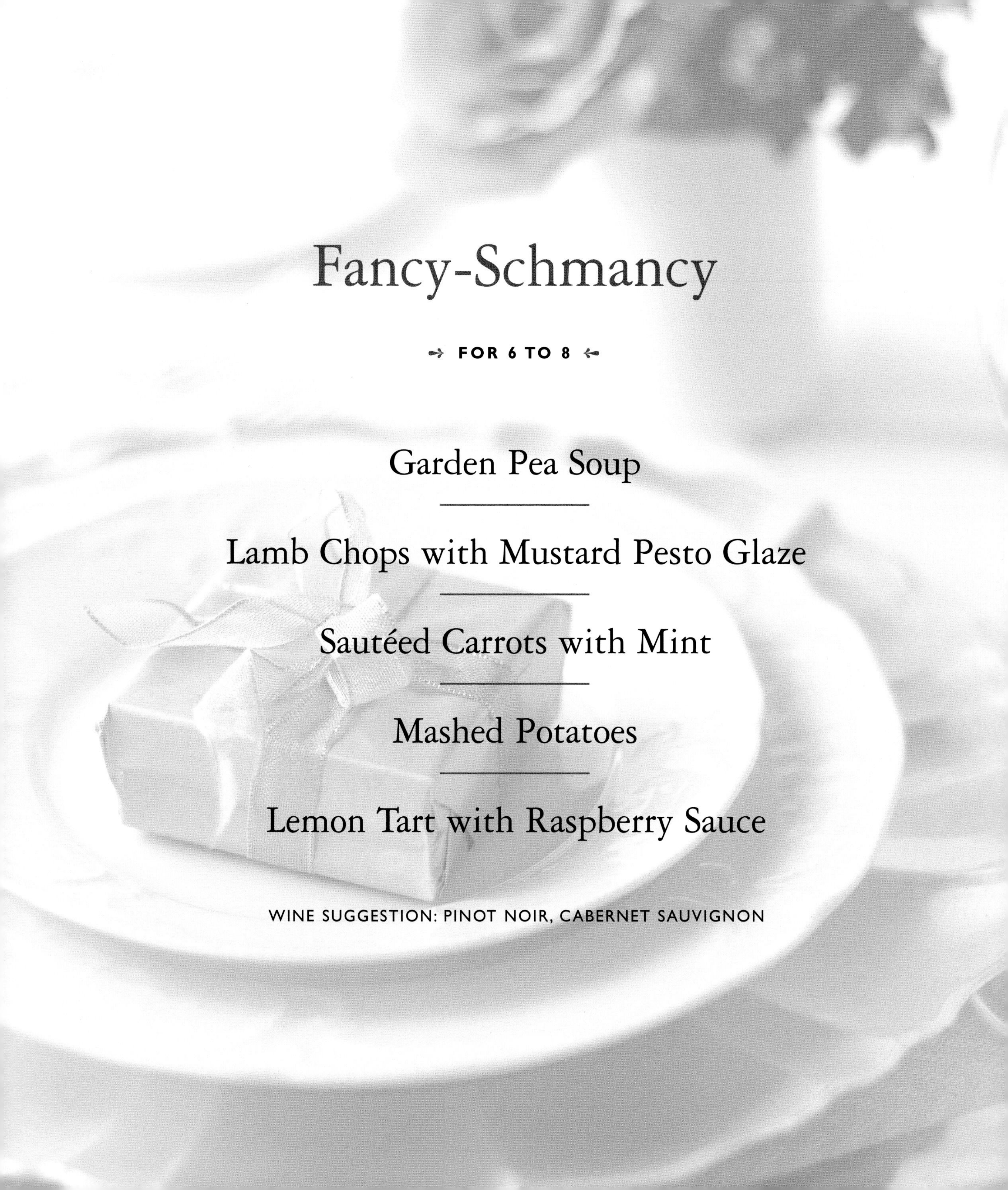

Fancy-Schmancy

Garden Pea Soup

———

Lamb Chops with Mustard Pesto Glaze

———

Sautéed Carrots with Mint

———

Mashed Potatoes

———

Lemon Tart with Raspberry Sauce

WINE SUGGESTION: PINOT NOIR, CABERNET SAUVIGNON

FANCY to look at, fancy to eat, but not fancy to make. Entirely doable in advance, and the only last-minute thing, apart from the reheating, is roasting the lamb chops.

SHORTCUT
A grocery or deli version of pea soup is certainly possible, ditto the cooked carrots (you add the mint) and mashed potatoes (you add extra butter and/or cream).

HOW TO DO IT:

❋ Make the soup, lemon tart, and raspberry sauce up to three days in advance.

❋ Marinate the lamb chops the day or night before. Let them come to room temperature before roasting.

❋ Prepare the carrots and potatoes and refrigerate. Let them come to room temperature before reheating (so their containers won't crack).

❋ About an hour before your guests arrive, take everything out of the fridge, except the soup, if you're serving it chilled. Now go get dressed and finish your last-minute fussing.

❋ Just before your guests arrive, serve the soup into individual bowls and have them ready to bring to the table.

❋ Tell your guests dinner is just about ready and nip into the kitchen for the 10 minutes or so it takes to broil the lamb chops and nuke the carrots and potatoes. The first person who says "Can I help you?" gets to put the soup on the table and feel special for doing it.

garden pea soup

SERVES 6 TO 8
PREP TIME: 10 MINUTES
COOKING TIME: 5 MINUTES

You know how I love color. Now you can have your color and eat it, too. (Ooh, did I say that?) Whatever, it's delicious!

* Place thawed peas, dill, salt, and pepper in a blender or a food processor and purée until smooth. Pour into a medium saucepan over medium-low heat. If you want a real velvety texture, strain the mixture through a sieve first, but we are usually too lazy.

* Stir in the half-and-half and simmer 5 minutes. Taste and adjust seasonings if necessary. Serve warm or chilled, with a dollop of sour cream and a sprig of fresh dill or sprinkling of chives, if you happen to have them.

VARIATION

Want to make this soup more substantial? Chop and sauté a small onion and fry 4 pieces of bacon. Crumble the bacon and add it and the onion to the soup. Serve hot. Mmmmm. You may also substitute chicken stock for half or even all the dairy, for a heartier flavor. Heavy cream would yield a richer texture; use skim milk for a dieter's version. A dash of hot sauce would zip things up, too.

TIP

Land-O-Lakes makes a fat-free half-and-half, and it is superb— can't tell the difference, I swear.

PREP:

Blender or food processor
Colander or sieve
Medium saucepan

Two 10-ounce packages frozen peas, thawed

3 tablespoons fresh chopped dill, or 1 tablespoon dried

1 teaspoon salt

½ teaspoon white pepper

1 pint half-and-half

Sour cream for garnish, if desired

Sprig of fresh dill or minced chives, for garnish, if desired

lamb chops with mustard pesto glaze

PREP:

Small bowl, plate, or pan just large enough
to hold chops while marinating
Baking pan
Aluminum foil

**Lamb chops about 1 inch thick, 2 or 3 per
person, depending on size and appetites**

Salt and ground black pepper

¾ cup prepared pesto sauce

¼ cup Dijon mustard

Olive oil or nonstick spray

SERVES 8
PREP TIME: 10 MINUTES
ROASTING TIME: 8 MINUTES FOR MEDIUM RARE

*I just can't say enough about store-bought pesto, and these lamb chops
are one of my favorite things to do with it. They are best prepared in
advance; the longer they marinate, the better.*

* Season the chops with salt and pepper. Mix the pesto and
mustard and slather the mixture on both sides of each lamb
chop. Cover with cling wrap and let marinate several hours or
overnight, if possible.

* Before baking, let the chops come to room temperature.
Meanwhile . . .

* Line the baking pan with aluminum foil and lightly grease
with olive oil or nonstick spray. Put the oven rack in the
topmost position, and heat the oven to broil. Or if you prefer,
prepare your grill.

* Broil about 4 minutes per side for rare, 5 minutes for
medium. This depends on the size of your chops, so check
them while cooking, just to be sure.

TIP

Lining your baking pans with aluminum foil, or better yet,
Reynolds Wrap Release, saves cleanup time. You just throw away
the foil and give the pan a quick soapy rinse if it needs it. Beats
scrubbing. *Love* that!

sautéed carrots with mint

PREP:

Microwavable glass baking dish
Cling wrap
Large frying pan

---

2 pounds prewashed baby carrots

¼ cup (½ stick) butter

**2 tablespoons chopped fresh mint,
or 2 teaspoons dried**

SERVES 6 TO 8
PREP AND COOKING TIME: 20 MINUTES

❋ Place the carrots in a microwavable dish. Add ⅓ cup water and cover with cling wrap. Microwave on high for 5 minutes, then let the carrots steam, covered, for about 1 minute. Test for doneness; they should be tender but not mushy. Cover again and cook longer if necessary, as cooking times vary according to the strength of your microwave.

❋ In a large pan over medium-high heat, melt the butter. Add the carrots and sauté for about 2 minutes, then sprinkle with mint. Serve warm or at room temperature.

mashed potatoes

**Instant mashed potatoes,
such as Hungry Jack**

¼ cup (½ stick) butter

**¾–1 cup milk or cream,
or as called for in package instructions**

SERVES 6 TO 8
PREP TIME: 10 MINUTES

First, I am all for buying these already prepared and then adding a little butter or cream and seasoning with salt and pepper to your taste. Second, if you can't buy them prepared, I find the instant ones pretty darn good. I'm not crazy about all the chemicals and junk in them, but I don't eat them every day, and the convenience is worth it. The packages usually call for margarine and milk, but I sometimes use real butter and cream, especially for special occasions. Treadmill, anyone? Oh, you also can make them ahead and reheat in the microwave, adding a little more milk or cream if necessary for desired consistency.

❋ Prepare according to package instructions, and you're done in a jiffy. Season to taste with salt and pepper.

lemon tart with raspberry sauce

MAKES ONE 9-INCH PIE OR 8 SMALL TARTS
PREP TIME: 20 MINUTES
COOKING TIME FOR CRUST: ABOUT 10 MINUTES
CHILLING TIME: 2 HOURS

I find commercial lemon curd to be very good but sometimes too sweet. Adding fresh juice and freshly grated zest makes it just right and makes it taste homemade. If you like it as it is, however, or you're really pushed, skip it. You could make this as one big tart or eight individual tarts using prepared tart shells. Another shortcut would be to skip the purée and simply sprinkle berries (any kind, fresh or frozen) with a few teaspoons of sugar and let them sit (macerate) until you're ready for them. Chilling the pie isn't mandatory, but it does give it a firmer consistency.

* Bake the pie crust according to package instructions, and let it cool completely.

* Taste the curd and then combine it with lemon juice and zest according to your taste.

* Spoon the curd into the prepared crust and refrigerate until serving time. Meanwhile . . .

* To make the purée, put the thawed raspberries into a blender or food processor and purée until smooth. Taste for sweetness and add sugar by teaspoonfuls until the mixture is sweet enough for you.

* To serve, spoon a little puddle of purée (or macerated berries) onto each plate and place the lemon tart on top, or place a tart serving on each plate and spoon berries and sauce over and around it.

PREP:

Medium bowl
9-inch pie or tart pan
Food processor or blender

One 9-inch pie crust

2 cups store-bought lemon curd, such as Wilkin and Sons

Juice and grated zest of 1 lemon, if desired

One 10-ounce package frozen raspberries, thawed

1 tablespoon sugar, or to taste

Acknowledgments

So, here you have it. What began as a simple idea between Frances and me, sitting in our jammies and chatting, has become my first in-home entertaining book. But, as always, nothing special happens alone. Although I headed the tablescaping team here in Los Angeles, it would not have come together without Jocelyne Borys and her creative team: Nathan Smith, Doug Scott, Steven Lee Burright. Kelly Johnston, our gal Friday (and the rest of the week) got everything where it was supposed to go and back again. Doug Hill remained the ever-flexible photographer, working with Adam Goodwin, our digital imaging consultant. Then, of course, there's my vital corporate team, Daniel J. Levin, Todd Optican, and the gal we call "glue," Sohayla Cude, all making sure that this book happened with as little daily disruption as possible. Our business manager, Gerri Leonard, and her team at Sendyk Leonard & Co. tracked the project financially with Shelly Gates, keeping daily watch for receipts. In New York, Frances Schultz did double duty, not only purging her private recipe file (boy, do I owe her) but also project managing and editing as well. Under her eye the food photography by Ben Fink and his team was simple and oh so chic. And the food testing by Laurie Woolever actually made great recipes spectacular. Then, of course, there's the Clarkson Potter publishing team, who continue to be great collaborators. Maggie Hinders used her enthusiasm and design skill to visually pull this book together while Rosy Ngo cracked the whip to assure that we got to press on time. And a very special and personal thanks to Lauren Shakely, who has been my champion and my publishing caretaker since day one—an enviable position I hope every author one day finds with their publisher. And lastly, thanks to the millions of viewers who have allowed me to be a part of their lives.

Index